Killer Housewives

Cynthia Elias

Published by Trellis Publishing, 2021.

KILLER HOUSEWIVES

First edition. July 2, 2021.

ISBN: 979-8224329595

Written by Cynthia Elias.

KILLER HOUSEWIVES

CYNTHIA ELIAS

Kim Hricko

Kim Hricko was getting ready to kill her husband the night they attended a Valentine's Murder Mystery Party. Kim was a woman who was intelligent and determined, the irony of the play's theme was not lost on her.

It was destiny calling.

She watched with rapt attention as the actors went through the motions. A wedding bride took out a blue vial and poured the "poisonous" contents into her groom's champagne glass.

She has the right idea, Kim thought.

Looking over at her husband Steve, she imagined him in the place of the actor on stage, choking to death.

Could it be that easy?

CHAPTER ONE

"Kim Hricko was one of those people that you look at and say 'I would never have guessed,'" forensic psychologist Paula Orange said. "Something inside her snapped when she wanted out of her marriage. It could have been so simple. Call a lawyer and file for divorce. Kim wanted a lot more than that. She wanted blood."

Steve and Kim Hricko would be introduced by their mutual friends Maureen and Mike Miller at Penn State in 1984. Their temperaments seemed to be the perfect complement to one another, they would have a yin-yang compatibility.

"Kim was a very gregarious personality," Maureen said. "She was very outgoing. Very friendly. Everybody liked her."

"Steve was my best friend since seventh grade," Mike said. "Corny as it sounds we were kinda each others brother that we didn't have. My wife had set up a double date. He (Steve) was smitten by her. Thought she was very attractive. Basically, they hit it off and from that point on started dating."

Steve was a burly figure at 6'3" and 245 lbs. He was a star college football player but was on the shy side.

"He was a big teddy bear," Maureen said. "He just wanted everybody that he loved to be happy and for him to take care of them."

Neither Kim or Steve dated much before their union. Kim had a distant relationship with her father after her own parents divorced. Her mother would remarry a man that would sexually and physically abuse her.

Steve and Kim would marry and have a daughter. Nine years into their marriage, Steve would still be smitten by the woman that the Millers had set him up with. Kim, however, would have feelings of resentment that built up over time.

Temperamentally, the couple did not match up well. Steve was an introvert. Kim an extrovert. Kim hung out with doctors and nurses while Steve just wanted to stay home. He didn't feel welcome into Kim's elite social circle, put off by their large houses and flashy cars.

But Steve remained in love with Kim despite that over the years she did not treat him with the same warmth as she once did. She was now cold and disinterested toward her spouse.

Steve blamed himself for the deterioration and began working to save his marriage.

His efforts would only serve to pour fuel on the fire...

CHAPTER TWO

Kim fed up with the loveless relationship, suggested that they get a divorce but Steve refused. He also dismissed the idea of counseling but after nine years he finally saw it as a last resort.

Steve went to counseling on his own and began taking steps to show Kim how much he truly cared. One of the first things he did was write his wife a long, heartfelt love letter.

Kim shared the letter with some of her friends who remarked at how beautiful it was. But Steve's words of love and devotion had no effect on Kim.

"Can you believe this shit?" Kim mocked as she read some passages aloud. "I am willing to do whatever it takes to save our marriage. It takes two of us. But I know we can do it. Together."

"I think that's sweet," her friend remarked.

"Gag me," Kim rolled her eyes. "Trust me, when you've been married as long as I have this kind of syrupy shit only makes you sick."

"I wish my husband would write me love letters."

"No," Kim said. "You don't. They keep coming and they don't stop. He's smothering me and following me around the house like a puppy dog."

Steve's renewed efforts to rekindle a long dead marriage were now being met with resentment. He was earnest in displaying his affection and becoming more communicative with Kim.

"Let's talk about our feelings," he said to his wife who stiffened with his every touch.

Kim would go to work eager to vent. She would open up about her marital difficulties to anyone who was willing to listen. She found a confidante in Jennifer Gowen.

"He is suffocating me," Kim told Gowen. "Stifling me. Following me around the damn house the whole time and cuddling with me at night. I can't even breathe. He's always asking me where I'm going or what I'm doing. Now he's calling me on my cell just to say 'Hi'. He never used to do that. It is annoying as shit."

But Steve was merely following the advise of his counsel. He had not dated much before Kim and she was his first serious relationship. He had no idea what to do when the relationship turned sour.

"It has to be said that Steve was on the receiving end of some very bad counseling advice," Orange said. "Appeasement never works and that is something that any decent psychiatrist or counselor should know. He kept turning the other cheek with Kim and that just fueled her resentment of him even more. This isn't to justify his murder, of course."

With his counseling session inspired efforts not yielding any results, Steve became distraught. He had done everything by the book but it wasn't working. He called his close friend Mike and opened up about his marriage and job difficulties.

"I don't know what to do, man," Steve said, his voice quaking with emotion. "I don't want to lose her. She's my life. My family is my everything. I feel like I've already lost her."

"Take it easy," Mike said. "We'll figure something out."

"What do you think I should do?" Steve asked.

"You need to take her out," Mike said "Someplace special. You know. Make a memory."

"Yeah," Steve said. "I know that. But I'm at a loss at how to go about it. I've tried everything."

"Tell you what," Mike said. "You come over to the Golf Resort."

"Harbourtowne?"

"I'll make sure you get the honeymoon cottage we have here. The very best one."

"You're too cool, Mike."

"Anytime, brother."

Mike worked at the Harbourtowne Golf Resort and set up the accommodations for his good friend and his wife. The place was hosting a Valentine's Day Murder Mystery play. Mike knew that the place worked wonders for romance. If there was anyplace that could rekindle the spark in a relationship, the resort would be it.

But Steve didn't know that Kim already had a romance of her own.

His name was Brad Winkler.

CHAPTER THREE

Kim had met Brad Winkler when she was planning out the bachelorette party for her co-worker, Jennifer Gowen. Jennifer had brought Brad to the wedding shower ahead of time and the United States Marine was the only man at the party aside from Steve.

Kim and the young man hit it off immediately. She gave him a ride home along with Norma Walz after the party was over. They dropped off Brad at his aunt's house and Kim watched from the car as the young man made his way inside.

"He was in a bad marriage," Kim said to Norma. "Pretty sad. He's a nice guy. Jesus. The girl who catches him is going to be a lucky one. He's really sweet."

Kim returned home and was chastised by Steve for spending so much time with Brad. He had no idea of the affair to come.

Jennifer Gowen would get married and enlist the aid of Brad to help around the house while she was away on her honeymoon. Jennifer had a one-year-old daughter and Brad would babysit the girl and do some chores around the place.

Kim would come over and help out with the baby on the day Gowen left.

The affair with Brad would begin that night. They would have their trysts at Jen's townhouse while his cousin was still on her honeymoon. When Jennifer returned, the couple would continue their affair at the home of Brad's aunt.

Kim was equally open about her affair with Brad Winkler among friends as she was about her dissatisfaction with her marriage.

"I'm seeing someone," Kim said to Rachel, her college friend.

"You're having an affair?"

"Its just sex," Kim said, shrugging her shoulder. "I'm not going to marry this guy."

Kim kept up the charade on the home front as she plotted her next move. The change in her behavior made Steve believe that his efforts were working as he chronicled in his journal.

"Life at home is improving," Steve wrote. "I am looking forward to Valentine's weekend at Harbourtowne with Kim. She called twice today and said 'I love you' without me saying it first. I was very happy. Kim and I have not made love yet and I want to but I will wait as long as it takes. I love her...I believe I know what being in love really is. We have been married nine years but I feel like we just started dating."

Sadly, four days after Steve wrote those words in his journal Kim was off buying Brad Winkler a Valentine's Day gift.

"Brad, I really want to give you all these gifts in person but I guess the Pentagon had a different idea," Kim wrote. "I am so proud of what you do so I'll just go on missing you. Have a nice weekend at home, baby. I look forward to seeing you soon. Happy Valentine's Day, sir. I love you so very much. Hugs and Kisses, Kim."

While Steve had an optimistic view of their future life together, Kim continued to tell anyone with a listening ear about her dissatisfaction.

"There is a lot of verbal abuse," Kim said to Theresa Armstrong, one of her neighbors. "From both of us. He doesn't do anything. I do everything. I am unhappy and don't want to be married to him anymore."

She then went to her job at Holy Cross Hospital and told her co-worker Norma Walz about her problems.

"I've been in a bad marriage for a long time," Kim said. "Me and Steve have been having problems for a long time. A very long time."

"I always suspected that something wasn't right," Norma said.

"I've been living a lie," Kim nodded. I wanted him to go to counseling two years ago. Now he's going. And he's driving me crazy."

Steve's constant fawning and pandering annoyed Kim so much that she began thinking about what life would be like without him.

"You know if my husband dies we'd be better off than if we got a divorce," Kim told one of her neighbors. "Steve doesn't make that much money. He's a groundskeeper. We get a divorce and I'm paying him alimony. But if he died, well, if he died we would inherit $450,000 from his life insurance."

"'That's a morbid thing to think about," the neighbor said, trying to laugh it off.

"You read about these stories all the time. The husband killing off the wife and vice-versa. I always wondered why they did it instead of just getting a divorce. It's the life insurance. Just like in the movies."

"What was lost in Kim's rationalizing was the fact that the killers most always get caught," Orange said. "But in her mind, she was the special one. Narcissists always think like that. Like they are the special one that won't get caught. Still, Kim needed that reassurance from her peers that she was doing the right thing as crazy as it sounds."

After not getting a receptive response from her neighbor, Kim once again turned to Jennifer Gowen.

"Steve would be better off dead," Kim said, using the same line on Jennifer. "We talked about getting a divorce but

Steve doesn't want that. Even if he did he is going to try and turn Anna against me or try to keep her. He doesn't have a life outside our marriage so he is better off dead anyway."

"You really shouldn't talk like that. Let alone think like that."

"Why not? I thought about telling him about Brad but I think he would just get depressed or suicidal. Then I would not be able to collect the insurance if he killed himself."

"You think he'd kill himself?"

"Probably," Kim said. "So I have to figure something else out. You know there was this serial killer. I forgot her name. But she would go around in the children's ward and shoot the kids up with Succinylcholine. It is a muscle paralyzer. No way to trace it."

Kim would later inform Gowen that if she could kill Steve and get away with it that she "would do it tomorrow."

Seeking other alternatives aside from poisoning, Kim approached fellow surgical tech Ken Burges in the locker room of the hospital.

"Hi, Ken."

"Hey there," Ken said.

"Do you know of anyone that could kill my husband?"

"What?" Ken asked. He thought Kim was playing a joke.

"Do you know anyone that can, you know, kill someone? For a price."

"I'm insulted that you would ask me that. Do I look that sketchy to you?"

Burges had been convicted of welfare fraud in Virginia a couple of years before obtaining his job at the hospital. Because of this, Kim may have presumed that he would be the type of person who would know people capable of such an act.

"I got $50,000 for anyone who could do something like that."

"You got the wrong dude," Ken said. "The wrong guy."

"Forget I even asked," Kim said.

"You work in the operating room," Ken advised. "You could just put him to sleep."

Ken didn't know that Kim already had that idea in mind.

Kim began to plot out details of the murder. She needed to do something that was untraceable. This called for poison. She had to burn away any evidence so her attack had to take place away from home.

She ran her plan by a college friend of hers, Rachel McCoy. Kim justified her actions by demonizing her husband. She talked about his unwillingness to do stuff with her as he was a homebody and kept a messy home. Their personalities were too different.

Then without warning, she began articulating her plan to kill Steve with the poison and then setting the place on fire.

It was almost as if she wanted Rachel to poke any holes in her plan should she miss anything.

Rachel tried to talk Kim out of the hare-brained idea to no avail. She suggested simply getting a divorce but Kim was convinced that killing Steve was "easier." Rachel also brought up the fact that she was robbing their daughter, Anna, of a father.

"She would be better off without him," Kim said.

Whatever Rachel suggested, Kim had an answer for.

Her mind was made up.

Steve had to go.

CHAPTER FOUR

Kim knew that the drug she had to obtain was Succinylcholine. It would be readily available to her as she did her rounds through the hospital. Just walk by a tray of meds in the surgery unit and lift one of the vials. Easy peasy.

"I'm going to get this drug," Kim told her friend Rachel. "It will paralyze Steve. Stop his breathing and then I'll set the curtains on fire with a candle or a cigar. He won't be able to move and then he'll die of smoke inhalation. Nobody will know shit."

Kim would not take into account the fact that her husband was a healthy and robust man with no medical history. That would certainly draw suspicion.

"This would be the only logical explanation for what brought about Steven Hricko's death," prosecuting attorney Robert Dean said. "Because there was nothing else wrong with him. His body organs were in fine shape, there was no trauma. It had to have been this. She had to have carried through her plan."

"Kim was determined," Orange said. "She wanted her cake and eat it too. It is a head scratcher as to why she didn't pursue a divorce but the mind of a sociopath works differently. She wanted a clean break. If she had gotten a divorce, then Steve would have remained in her life forever the next ten years because of their daughter. She wanted to erase him from the picture and nothing and nobody was going to talk her out of it."

The planned romantic getaway loomed on the horizon for Valentine's Day weekend. Steve looked forward to their alone time together with giddy excitement. He told his counselor that this would be the turning point where the sparks of romance would once again be rekindled.

But Kim looked toward the weekend with dread. She had told Jennifer Gowen that she had only had sex with Steve once in the past six months and the experience left her feeling repulsed.

"I'm not looking forward to the trip," Kim said in her own counseling session.

"Why?" her counselor asked. "It may be an opportunity to rekindle some passion."

"I'm tired and really don't feel up to the trip. It's a long drive. It is going to be miserable."

Then a light bulb flashed in Kim's mind. The resort would be the perfect place.

The perfect place to put her plans into effect.

CHAPTER SIX

Valentine's Day weekend arrived.

Steve had romance on his mind. His forehead perspired as he felt the anxiety of trying to save his marriage.

Kim had Brad Winkler on her mind as she looked out the car window.

Then her mind drifted to murder.

She had to set everything up just right. Inject Steve. Burn the cottage room. Then tell the police her story and stick with it no matter what.

Kim and Steve drove from their home in Laurel, Maryland to St Michaels. It would be a 75-mile to a romantic getaway that many had christened as the "Heart & Soul of Chesapeake Bay."

But the couple arrived at their cottage and found the place to be freezing. Kim started a fire in the wood stove then made some coffee.

The conversation was muted and awkward. They decided to watch some TV before looking out the window and taking in the view of the bay. It was windy and the the cold, damp weather chased them back inside

Preparing for the dinner, Steve popped a few Effexor tablets for his depression which had gotten worse in recent weeks. He also took an anti-anxiety medication called Xanax and a muscle relaxant called Flexeril.

Getting dressed, they attended the interactive murder mystery dinner called THE BRIDE WHO CRIED. The actors staged a re-enactment of a woman killing her soon to be husband. The actors encouraged audience members to ask the actors questions in an attempt to find out who the murderer was.

Kim enjoyed the play immensely. When the actors called for audience participation, she was one of two women who went out onto the stage and began asking questions like a detective.

The play now over, Kim and Steve returned to their cottage. Not yet having their fill of entertainment, the couple would watch the comedy film "Tommy Boy". They got a good laugh out of it but according to Kim they "still did not talk about our problems."

Steve then fell asleep.

Kim stood over him like a predator then went to the bathroom to prepare her lethal cocktail of succinylcholine. Building up her nerve, she finally did the move that she had been practicing in her head for two years.

Kim pulled aside the bed sheet and injected the syringe into his neck.

I'll burn the body. That will get rid of the puncture wound.

Kim also knew that the drug she administered only caused paralysis. It didn't affect a patient's level of consciousness.

So when Kim set the room on fire, Steve would know that he was being burned to death.

And he wouldn't be able to do anything about it.

The thought made Kim smile. She didn't want to just kill him. She wanted to make him suffer. To humiliate him.

Kim pulled the now paralyzed but awake Steve off the bed and dropped him to the floor. She doused his body with lighter fluid.

Kim, what are you doing? Steve looked up at his wife, unable to move or speak.

"Call it the perfect crime," she whispered in his ear as if reading his thoughts.

He stared straight up at the ceiling, catching Kim's movements in the corner of his eye.

He heard a matchstick strike against a box.

Then he felt a sharp pain race up his body as she set him ablaze.

I can't move, Steven thought as terror and pain engulfed him.

I can't breathe.

I can't breathe.

Kim, what are you doing?

I brought you here to save our marriage. I have done what I could do making this better.

I love you. Please don't do this!

Kim poured more of the lighter fluid onto Steve's body. She lit another match and threw it on him.

"She injected him with succinylcholine and watched him suffocate," Maureen said. "And lit him on fire. How much colder could it get."

CHAPTER FIVE

Kim Hricko walked into the resort reception area with a calm demeanor. She had her ear to her cell phone which was turned upside down.

"I need to talk to someone who works here," she informed desk clerk Elaine Phillips.

"I work here," Elaine said, expecting Kim's response being anything from wanting more towels to complaining about faulty air conditioning.

"My room is on fire."

"Is there anyone else in the room?" Phillips asked.

"Yeah," she said without emotion. "My husband."

"What room are you in?" Elaine asked, making her way around the corner of the desk.

Elaine and another hotel employee hurried into the courtyard of the resort.

"You smell that?" Elaine asked. "Something is definitely burning."

The two sprinted to cottage number 506 at the end of the resort. The door was shut but there was a tiny opening in the sliding door in the rear.

Smoke filled the room. They could barely see one foot in front of them. Kneeling down, one of the employees saw the the prone figure of a man inside. He crawled in, braving the smoke and pulled the body to safety on the back porch.

It was too late.

Steve Hricko, burned to a crisp.

The man had died with a Playboy magazine at his side with his pajama pants down at his knees as if he collapsed while masturbating.

"I want to see his dead body," Kim said as she milled around with the hotel guests watching the scene.

"I thought it was odd," one of the guests said. "Because no one had pronounced anyone to be dead yet."

Kim gave her statement to the Sheriff then called their best friends, Mike and Maureen Miller.

"It's the last thing you expect when you receive a phone call at night," Maureen said. "When the phone rings at night you know that it's not anything good."

"My wife answered the phone," Mike Miller said. "And sort of roused me a little bit and said that there's was an incident in Steve and Kim's room. Kim's requesting that you come down there as soon as possible.

The Millers were shocked at the sudden death of Steve. They were even more shocked at the demeanor of Kim when they went to console her.

"I didn't expect her to be anything less than a hysterical woman whose husband passed away," Maureen said. "She was the exact opposite. Just exact opposite."

Kim told everyone that Steve was drunk and made advances toward her. He groped and fondled her but she didn't want to have sex. They argued and she left the cottage.

Mike knew that something was fishy. His friend Steve was not a drinker.

Did Kim plan this out?

"They said the fire started because of him carelessly smoking," Mike said. "Steve doesn't smoke. All the years I've known Steve, I've never seen him smoke a cigarette, a cigar. He despised being around people that smoked."

An autopsy was performed and forensic pathologist Janis Amatuzio, like Mike Miller, quickly realized that something was amiss.

"Steven's body was found in a fire," Amatuzio said. "The major question for the forensic pathologist is that did he die of the fire or not. When there was no soot in the airways, when there was no damage to the lungs. It suggested that Steven was dead before the fire started."

"Steven was not drunk that night," prosecuting attorney Robert Dean said. "The drug tests and the autopsy shows that. Steve was not drunk."

The picture didn't fit. Steve was not a drinker nor was he a smoker. But friends and family could not believe the worst about Kim Hricko. The fun and outgoing mother could not have killed her own husband, the man who adored her for the past nine years.

Could she?

"Was she really capable of doing this?" Maureen asked. "Everybody was saying it but again, I ignored it and just pushed it back and said that she wasn't capable of doing it. Man, was I wrong."

CHAPTER SIX

Police began their investigation and discovered that Kim left a trail of incriminating conversations as well as evidence.

"Kim was too smart for her own good," Orange said. "She did her research on succinylcholine, did her research on the how quickly a body burns. But she did not know how to stage a killing."

Kim had left empty beer bottles in the room and a pack of cigars. The cigars would be the clue that blew Kim's story up in smoke.

Steve was not a smoker and the cigars she had left behind as evidence were not the kind to start a fire.

"There was an investigation as to how a fire like this could have started," prosecuting attorney Robert Dean said. "That fire could not have started by the ashes of a cigar."

Kim would state that after she and Steve had gotten into a fight she went for a drive. She wanted to visit Mike and Maureen Miller who only lived minutes away. She stated she had become lost. The prosecution thought that her excuse seemed odd as she had visited the Millers on numerous occasions. She also had a brother who lived only a few blocks away from the Miller home. And why had she not simply called them on her cell phone?

"I didn't want to wake anyone," Kim said when asked why she didn't call.

Her answer was incongruent as why would she worry about waking someone up with a cell phone call when she didn't have a problem arriving on their doorstep in the middle of the night?

Nine days after the murder, police would arrive at the home of a Hricko friend where Kim had been staying. They had a search warrant for her car but Kim felt the noose tightening around her neck. She ran to the bathroom room and locked it behind herself as the police entered the home.

Kim then swallowed a whole bottle of Xanax.

"Come out of there, Kim," the police yelled.

They busted the door down and saw Kim there in the bathtub, holding a razor blade over her wrist.

"I'll kill myself!" she screamed. "I'll fucking do it!"

The officers quickly subdued Kim without further incident. They then transported her to a psychiatric facility where she was put on suicide watch.

The trial would only last six days as the prosecuting attorney detailed how Kim staged the murder.

"She stated that he was sloppy drunk," prosecuting attorney Robert Dean said. "And that he wanted to have sex. She said they got into an argument and that she left for a few hours. She said she drove around and got lost. And then she returned to the cottage and saw that it was full of smoke and then she reported that the room was on fire."

The case against Kim was made by several friends, co-workers, and neighbors. They all testified about the affair, the plot to kill Steve and her desire to acquire the drug succinylcholine.

Kim Hricko would be found guilty of murder and arson. She would be sentenced to life in prison.

"It's sad that he (Steve) is not the one in the world anymore and she is," Maureen said.

"He was my best friend," Mike said. "And the fact that he isn't here anymore is pretty hard for me to take."

The other victim aside from Steve was their nine-year-old daughter. She lost both her father and her mother.

"Her child is the victim," Maureen said. "And is forever going to wonder which side of the family is telling the truth. Is it true that her mother was unjustly accused or is it true that she's a cold, manipulating, calculating murderer."

END

HUSBAND KILLER : THE TRUE STORY OF MICHELLE HALL

24

TORI BAKER

It's never easy being a member of a blended family. There's a certain understanding that comes along with a second or third marriage – especially one involving children – that there is going to be a fundamental need for combined effort, tolerance and compromise.

When Michelle Garner remarried for what would be the third and last time, family and friends believed she had finally found happiness after reconnecting with an old high-school flame.

John Brittson "Britt" Hall, an aircraft mechanic and home builder, had known his own fair share of heartache; he was recently divorced when he found his old high school girlfriend, Michelle, on an online dating web site.

Britt Hall and Michelle Garner first met in 1986 while attending high school in Newnan, GA. The two briefly dated before Michelle Hall graduated in 1987.

"They both were in the popular clique," forensic psychologist Robert Brion said. "Britt was a baseball player that all of the girls had a crush on. Michelle was popular herself, very outgoing with a lot of friends."

The parents of Britt and Michelle were friends as well but they didn't consider the dating relationship between Michelle and Britt to be a serious one. After graduation, Michelle would move away and she would marry a man named Rusty Hart. The couple would have two daughters until their divorce in 1996.

The single mom worked as a dental assistant to support her daughters. Times were tight until 1999 when she met and married Steve Davis.

"Steve Davis was a businessman," Brion said. "He was divorced himself with a daughter of his own. He met Michelle and quickly fell for her charms as she could come across as a very warm and caring person. He asked her to marry him after about a year of dating."

Michelle would become pregnant during the union and give birth to her third daughter, Alyssa.

Unfortunately, her second marriage met the same fate as her first and within a few years, the couple had filed for divorce, citing irreconcilable differences.

Britt did well for himself after high school, becoming an airline mechanic for Delta Airlines. He made good money with Delta until they laid him off. He then went into business with his father in home construction until ultimately returning back to Delta after they had a rehire.

His marriage started to fail, however. His first wife cited that Britt had "mental problems" and filed for divorce, stating that the marriage was "irretrievably broken."

"Britt's first wife would take him to court at least six to eight times a year after their divorce," Brion said. "He was depressed and the court visits weren't helping."

His divorce would coincide with Michelle's impending divorce with Steve Davis. Her divorce with Davis was a particularly nasty one and Britt could sympathize. They would reconnect over a dating website.

In the midst of her own divorce, Garner was happy to find love again with Britt Hall as they rekindled old flames. Shortly after reconnecting, Britt invited Michelle over for Sunday lunch with his family, and all seemed well for the couple.

"Michelle did mention to Britt's family that she was going through some difficult times with her divorce," Brion said. "She was cheerful throughout but hinted that the custody battles she was going through were quite serious."

Little did Britt Hall's family know that their excitement would soon be turned to devastation; a tragedy that would make national headlines and be detailed in various murder documentaries.

THE BRADY BUNCH

Ronald Hall, Britt's father was all to happy to have Michelle back in his son's life. At least at first.

"We visited and talked," Ronald said. "And she came in and was just as happy as she ever was," he said.

It wasn't long before Britt Hall's romance with Garner turned more serious, and the two tied the knot in September of 2006. The new marriage was an adjustment, to say the least. Britt had three children from his previous marriage and Michelle Hall had three of her own children as well. The blended family of eight was now living in Britt Hall's town home.

"You can imagine how tight the living quarters were," Brion said. "But Michelle's girls really took to their new stepfather. They became comfortable enough to call him 'Dad'."

Britt wanted a bigger home and decided to build a large home with the help of his father. The men paid for contractors to pour concrete and establish the foundation, but father and son built the majority of the house by hand.

"People didn't know where the couple were getting the money to build the house," Brion said. "But Britt did most of the work himself after the foundation was laid. So he was able to save a lot of money when it came to sweat equity. That's a testimony to how badly he wanted the marriage between he and Michelle to work out."

When all was said and done, Britt and Michelle Hall were the proud owners of a beautiful 4100 square foot home on ten acres, the perfect place to spend the rest of their lives together. The brand new house boasted vaulted ceilings, granite counter tops, and a finished basement. The construction would prove to be a house of cards, however, as things were brewing underneath the surface.

Michelle didn't have much luck with her two previous marriages, and although individual accounts may vary, her two former husbands are both to have reported being abused by Michelle during the course of their marriage.

Michelle never had a firm grasp on her emotions and didn't handle anger well. These character flaws would not bode well for her life with

Britt. Dealing with both partners' ex-spousal issues including custody and visitation, Michelle and Britt found themselves tinkering on the edge of divorce after a few months into their marriage.

"The way Britt and Michelle handled their issues were different," said family friend Sue Mathis. "Michelle was quicker to speak her mind and a lot of times, Britt just wanted her to try to gain a little bit more self-control."

Dealing with his own ex-wife and their similar divorce problems, Britt Hall was also facing his own internal battles with depression. Although he wasn't often the instigator in their frequent arguments, he was known to fervently engage in the verbal conflicts. While this certainly wasn't conducive to a happy and fruitful marriage, Britt Hall made it clear to friends he would not give up on his family and the life he had built.

The next couple of years came with continued stress, intensified by financial worries after the Halls realized they had gotten too far deep in debt as a result of building their dream home. Notices of foreclosure, liens on the house, and over-extensions were haunting the couple and causing both spouses to hit a breaking point.

On July 30, 2008, it was another typical tense day in the Hall household. Friends say Britt Hall, already aggravated due to a landscaper failing to complete a job on time, went to the store to pick-up hot dogs for a family get-together.

"Hey hon," Britt said as he called his wife. "How many hot dogs do you think I should get-"

"Count how many damn people are here," Michelle snapped. "That's how much you should get."

This would be the snide comeback that would break the straw in Britt's back. He grew tired at her constant bickering and baiting. When he came home that evening, a fight would ensue.

Michelle's youngest daughter, Alyssa, was in the living room watching television as her mother vacuumed to prepare for the company soon arriving. When Britt Hall told Alyssa to turn the TV down, another argument between the couple ensued and Hall immediately told her daughter to go upstairs to her bedroom and not come out until she was called.

There are only two individuals who know the details of what followed on that evening, and only one of them lived to tell. When all was said and done, Britt would be dead and Michelle would be charged with murder.

The 911 call came in at 8:02 p.m. by a frantic Michelle who told dispatchers that her husband had tried to kill her and commit suicide.

"He shot at me, and we were fighting to get it," Michelle told dispatchers regarding the weapon. She said she heard the gun go off twice. Seconds later, she told dispatchers her husband was turning blue.

When police arrived, Britt Hall was dead and had three noticeable gunshot wounds to his body: one on his left arm, one on his right thigh, and a close-range shot to his chest. Michelle Hall, bruised, scraped and covered in blood, told first responders the same story she had told dispatchers: her suicidal husband had tried to kill her before turning the gun on himself.

Prior to further investigation, deputies on the scene immediately called Britt Hall's parents and told them their son had committed suicide. The Halls refused to believe the news.

"Things just seemed to be going too good at this time in his life for him to have done that," said his mother, Charlene Hall. "I knew he didn't kill himself; I knew for a fact that didn't happen."

It didn't take long for police to begin seeing the crime scene a little differently than Michelle had described. Blood splatter and numerous bullet holes covered the downstairs bedroom, and a trail of blood led into the bathroom where Britt Hall's lifeless body now lay. If this was a suicide, there sure was a struggle beforehand.

Investigators gave Michelle the opportunity to explain the scene. She told how an argument between the couple turned violent when

Britt Hall threw her onto the bed. He immediately went into the study and she followed him.

Then she noticed the gun on the computer desk.

Knowing her husband was battling depression, she said she immediately became concerned with his safety, worried that he may use the gun to harm himself.

Michelle stated that she instinctively dove for the gun, and that's when Britt Hall reached for it as well and the two began struggling for possession.

After both Michelle and her husband lost control of he gun, she quickly picked up the weapon and began shooting rounds into the walls and floor in an effort to unload the gun.

In the hall, Britt Hall caught up with her and that's when she said he threatened to kill her. In yet another entanglement of an attempt for control of the gun, Michelle said the gun accidentally went off. This shot punctured Britt Hall's thigh, and that's when Hall claimed she went to call for help.

Britt Hall began crawling into the bathroom, unable to walk and calling out her name for help. When she approached him, gun in hand, she said he grabbed the pistol from her, put it to his chest, and pulled the trigger.

The problem with her story, however, was that most suicides don't entail multiple gunshot wounds. Additionally, the manner in which the fatal shot was delivered raised eyebrows for investigators.

"I've worked many suicides in my career, and I've never worked a suicide that I can remember where a man had shot himself in the chest," Lt John Lewis said.

Furthermore, the gunshot wound on Britt Hall's chest had no signs of charring or burning around the entry wound, signs which usually indicate a self-inflicted wound.

Britt Hall also had a shattered elbow and a bullet hole in his left arm. Three different shots, all which led investigators to believe they weren't being told the whole story.

Michelle did her best to persuade the investigative team to believe her story, but her story changed upon being brought to the station for questioning. While at first she claimed the two struggled for control over the gun, she then claimed Britt Hall was never actually in possession of the gun at all.

Coupled with the evidence at the crime scene and her story's inconsistencies, Michelle was charged the next morning with the murder of her husband.

Crucial to the prosecution's case was the testimony of Michelle's youngest daughter, Alyssa, who was in the home during the shooting. Police brought the 8-year-old in for questioning immediately following the incident and she clearly stated she heard her step-father pleading with her mother to "put the gun down," she said. Alyssa would ultimately testify in her mother's trial in 2009.

Facing charges of malice murder and aggravated assault, Michelle vehemently denied killing her husband. She insisted that he died of a self-inflicted gunshot wound after threatening suicide and fighting with her over the .38 caliber revolver.

The fight that evening was par for the course, she said. The two regularly got into verbal and physical altercations, and their marriage was falling apart due to financial stress. They would also constantly fight over ex-spouses, custody and visitation regarding the six children. Although there were no police reports relating to any domestic altercations in the home before, family and friends knew things weren't okay on the home front.

"Britt would spend several nights driving to work calling me and saying 'I don't know what to do.' He would have done everything in his power to save his marriage, even if it was not worth saving. He was terrified of failure," said Mathis.

One of the first fights that turned physical in front of the family was in November 2006, when Britt Hall's eldest daughter came into the room to find Michelle Hall unconscious. Her father quickly ushered her out of the room and told her not to worry about it. The next couple of years only brought more trouble due to the same old problems and Britt's alleged mental illness.

Britt was prescribed three different types of medication for depression at the time of his death, police confirmed.

But the physical evidence did not add up to suicide. Initially, the Georgia Bureau of Investigation estimated the fatal gunshot to have been fired from around 18-24 inches away. This is not consistent with suicide, detectives argued. While many victims of mental illness fall prey to suicide each year, the facts must add up. In this case, they did not.

If convicted, Michelle was facing life in prison.

In September of 2009, testimonies were heard by Alyssa Davis, as well as responding officers Capt. Tony Grant and Sgt. Freddy Cox, about what they saw and heard on the night of the shooting.

Cox testified that Hall's appearance was "consistent with someone who'd been in a physical altercation" and that Hall had bruises, scrapes and blood on her neck and forehead as well as blood on her hands and a knot on her elbow.

During his testimony, Grant stated he immediately noticed that Hall's face was red and she had what appeared to be gun-shot residue on her hand, even though she was stating her husband had committed suicide.

There were multiple bullet holes throughout the downstairs of the home when police arrived on the scene, Grant testified. Two bullets were recovered from Britt Hall's body and three more were found in the house.

Grant said a blood pattern analysis showed blood spatters of 90 degrees in the downstairs quarters outside of the bathroom, proof that Britt Hall crawled into the bathroom after being wounded.

Defense Attorney Mike Kam said that while in no uncertain terms would he call the key ear witness a liar, her age and her location during the shooting did not make for the most reliable testimony.

"She was eight; she didn't see anything, she clearly got some of the facts confused." Kam said in an interview. "She's not someone who is used to being asked questions in formal interview settings. Who knows what she remembered, or what happened?"

Additionally, Kam indicated that Michelle certainly didn't fit the description of a murderer. Outside of two divorces, Hall had no criminal record. She was law-abiding citizen, with nothing in her background which would give the assumption she was capable of murder, he said.

But the jury had heard enough. On September 25, 2009, Michelle Hall was found guilty on all counts in the death of her husband Britt.

Not long after her conviction, Hall's attorneys filed a motion for a new trial, citing trial court errors. Coweta County Superior Court Judge Jack Kirby denied the motion and the defense attorneys took the case to the Supreme Court.

On September 22, 2010, the Supreme Court of Georgia upheld the conviction, despite Hall's defense's argument that the trial court erred by admitting similar transaction evidence and prior consistent statements.

Hall's defense stated that testimony from both of her ex-husbands that she was verbally and physically abusive were inadmissible because they were not "sufficiently similar" to establish proof of the crimes for which she was charged, according to the opinion of the Supreme Court. It also stated that "in cases of domestic violence, prior incidents of abuse against family members or sexual partners are more generally permitted because there is a logical connection between violent acts against two different persons with whom the accused had a similar emotional or intimate attachment."

The opinion also added that the fifteen and thirteen-year lapses of time between her ex-husband's allegations of abuse to the alleged shooting of her husband did not require exclusion of evidence.

"Given that the similar transaction evidence reflects appellant's behavior towards prior spouses, we conclude that any prejudice from the age of these prior incidents was outweighed by the probative value of the evidence under the particular facts of this case and the purpose for which the similar transactions were offered."

Eighteen months later, however, Michelle retained a new attorney who filed a habeas corpus petition, stating Michelle was given ineffective legal counsel by Kam during her trial in 2009. Senior Judge Robert B. Struble presided over the hearing and determined that Hall was in-fact entitled to a new trial. Struble agreed that Kam, Hall's trial attorney, was "ineffective and fell below the minimum guarantee of representation under the constitution," a press release said.

While Michelle may have been looking forward to another chance at redemption, The Attorney General's Office quickly announced their plans to appeal the habeas corpus ruling to the Georgia Supreme Court.

In a press release on March 30, 2012, Coweta County District Attorney Peter John Skandalakis expressed his respectful disapproval of the court's ruling and that in stating Kam was ineffective for representation, "the court erroneously applied the wrong standard under the law."

Skandalakis said he was optimistic that the Supreme Court will conclude that Hall had a legally sufficient defense and that her conviction would be upheld after review of the appeal.

On January 22, 2013, the Supreme Court found Hall's convictions to be fair and just, denying insufficient representation during her 2009 trial. According to the court summary, the Supreme Court concluded that the habeas corpus petition did not conduct proper legal analysis to determine the effectiveness of Hall's defense.

The opinion references Strickland v. Washington, a 1984 Supreme Court case in which it determined that to be granted a new trial, a defendant must show that it was due to insufficient performance by defense that the defendant was found guilty.

Michelle's argument for her habeas corpus petition was that "if she were in the same room when her young daughter was questioned, she could have assisted her attorney by prompting him with specific information," the court says in its opinion. However, it was determined during the habeas hearing that any information she would have portrayed to her attorney was already known information to both parties. "As such, Hall has failed to show actual prejudice, and her claim of ineffective assistance of counsel should have been rejected," the opinion said.

Today, Michelle Hall remains in a Coweta County prison.

Since her conviction, Michelle's ex-husbands have been given full custody of her three respective daughters.

She won't be eligible for parole until 2039. She will be 70 years old.

SERIAL KILLING MOM : THE TRUE STORY OF STACEY CASTOR

36

PAULA ANTHONY

Stacey Ruth Castor may have been one of the most sociopathic female serial killers in modern times. She poisoned her first husband Michael Wallace with anti-freeze after he becomes an inconvenience to her and did the same to her second husband David Castor years later. When she caught wind that the police were onto her methods, she poisoned her own daughter and wrote 'confession' letter on her behalf.

She tried to pin the crimes on her daughter.

Dubbed the Black Widow by the national media, recent findings have opened up the possibility that Stacey killed her own father as well.

Cool, calm and collected, Stacey maintained her innocence throughout the court proceedings, adamantly pointing the finger of blame at her own daughter. But what possessed her to kill not only her husbands but her own flesh and blood?

This is her story.

EARLY LIFE

Stacey was born July 27th, 1967 in Clay, New York. She would meet what she called the 'love of her life' in a bar at age seventeen.

His name was Michael Wallace.

"There was some kind of bet going on," Stacey's daughter, Ashley Wallace said. "He (Michael) had bet a friend that he would take her home that night. Then after that night they were together."

Stacey stated that she knew within the first five minutes of meeting Michael that she would marry him.

Michael was six years older than Stacey. He was loud and gregarious, always laughing and looking for a good time. This was a contrast to the personality of Stacey who was more withdrawn and kept people at arm's length. Michael brought her out of her shell.

"He was like something out of the 'Dukes of Hazzard'," Michael's brother-in-law Jonathon Corbett said. "He was all about yee-haw! Let's go have a beer. Just for fun. Let's go for a ride. Just for fun."

It would take five years for the couple to marry as they tied the knot at Stacey's parent's home.

Michael was a happy go lucky guy. But this happiness was fueled by drugs and alcohol according to Stacey.

"He had a problem with both for a long time in his life," Stacey recalled.

Michael would be arrested on numerous occasions for DUI. Finally, the judge got fed up and sent him to jail for a short period of time.

After he got out of jail, Michael vowed to change his ways. The couple married and Stacey would give birth to their first daughter, Ashley, in 1988.

"I knew from that minute on, my whole reason for being here was to take care of her," Stacey said.

Three years later, they would welcome another daughter, Bree.

Stacey would work as a dispatcher for an ambulance company while Michael worked nights as a mechanic. Times were hard financially but their contrast in personalities look to do them in. They would fight but it would not be about money because according to Stacey, "they had none."

PARENTAL FAVORITISM

Among their many disputes, Stacey would accuse Michael of favoring the youngest daughter Bree over everyone else. He would call Bree his "little princess" while paying less attention to Ashley. Stacey said that she made up for this perceived favoritism by becoming closer to Ashley.

"Bree was daddy's little angel," Stacey's friend Dani Colman said. "She could do no wrong. There was no talk of any relationship between Ashley and Michael Wallace."

The couple would continue to grow apart over the years and each was rumored to have had affairs. Still, their weakening marriage didn't seem to affect the children as both daughters remembered their childhood with a fondness.

"We'd just go for a ride in the car, you know?" Bree said. "For no reason, just take a ride. That was fun."

But by 1999, the couple were at odds on a daily basis. Suddenly, Michael began feeling sick. Over the holidays, his family members would describe him as having an unsteady gait and looking bloated. More than one person suggested that he see a doctor.

Michael would die in early 2000 with only eleven-year-old Ashley present in the room. She noticed he was sick but didn't think to call the doctor.

"He was laying on the couch, making what I thought were funny faces," Ashley said. "And all of sudden, he just sticks his arm up in the air and puts his arm on his side and then his arm just fell down."

Ashley left her father on the couch and went to pick up her sister Bree from school. "I've relived this day over and over again in my head, because what if there was something that I could've done?" Ashley recalled . "Like, I should've known, but I didn't. I was 11!"

Doctors would tell Stacey that Michael died of a heart attack. Michael's sister, however, held her suspicions about his demise.

"The color of his skin from head to chest was deep, dark purple," Michael's sister, Rosemary Corbett said. And it was really weird."

She wanted an autopsy but Stacey steadfastly refused.

"Stacey knew how to cover her tracks," forensic psychiatrist Paula Orange said. "Her mistakes came later in her serial killer career. And she was a serial killer, make no mistake about that. She didn't kill so much for profit or money. She killed out of convenience. When something wasn't going her way and she had to eliminate someone, she would do it without remorse or feeling."

THE GRIEVING PROCESS

Stacey took her two daughters and did her best to try and move on with their lives. She treated the girls to a trip to Disney World to try and put some happiness back in their life. Her gestures seemed empty to the children as she continued to hold things in and became colder to her children.

"My mom was never really around (after Michael died)," Ashley said. "I did all of the things she was supposed to do. I took care of my sister."

KILLING DAD

Stacey was also rumored to have been behind the murder of her father, Jerry Daniels, in February of 2002.

Michael's brother in law, John Corbett, found out that Daniels was hospitalized for a lung ailment. His condition was improving until his daughter Stacey visited.

Daniels would day soon after her visit and Corbett recalled Stacey giving him a can of soda for him to drink.

Stacey then had her father cremated and took control over his estate.

NEW HUSBAND

Stacey would start dating again, settling on David Castor. David was the polar opposite of Michael. He didn't party, didn't drink and had his own business. He had a stability that Stacey always wanted.

"He had money," Ashley said. "And my Mom was happy with that."

"He was attracted to Stacey because she accepted him," David Castor Jr said. "I think he just wanted someone there with him."

The new couple looked like peas in a pod. David had red hair just like Janice. He also had a thick, out of style mustache just like Michael Wallace before him. He looked like a scaled down version of Chicago Bear football coach Mike Ditka and had the fiery personality to match.

David had been married before to Janice Poissant. The two had a child together, David Jr, and had a happy marriage until David suffered a head injury during a motorcycle accident. He experienced amnesia for a long period of time and eventually got his memory back. His personality changed, however, and he would be a lot more brusque in his demeanor. He would soon prefer material goods over people. He would verbally abuse Janice until she finally decided to leave him after twenty-six years of marriage.

David had his own air conditioning installation and repair company which he purchased from Janice's father. His father-in-law had taught him everything about the business from the ground up. Janice and mother-in-law would work in the office while he went out on service calls. After his marriage to Janice ended, David's business began to flounder. His father-in-law bailed him out, however, and helped him put the business back on its feet.

Stacey would eventually replace Janice not only in marriage but in the business as well, becoming his office manager.

David didn't have Michael's substance abuse problems but he loved his toys. He would purchase motorcycles, jet skis, snowmobiles, and boats. His spending habits would cause a rift with his wife.

"They did fight because my Mom paid the majority of the bills," Ashley said. "And David just paid for his toys."

The marriage of blended families would cause a rift between the children. The girls did not take kindly to David's personality. He thought his controlling ways would keep the girls in line. Instead, his rules and regulations had the opposite effect.

The girls would rebel.

"At first, we didn't get along at all," Ashley said.

David had issues with the girls. He didn't allow his first wife an allowance and made it clear to the girls that he was the man "large and in charge."

Ashley would stand up to him first. She was older than Bree and had the bigger mouth. Stacey would intervene and do her best to try and make the girls see the positive benefit of living with David. They were closer to their school and had a bigger house.

The girls, however, had gotten used to being a threesome.

"David made it very clear that he didn't want any more kids," Bree recalled. "He didn't want to be our father and he didn't want to act like it."

He would send the teenage girls mixed signals, on one hand giving them the cold shoulder but on occasion trying to be their friend.

David and Ashley did eventually mend their ways as when she graduated from school she saw the 'proud father' look on his face.

"He wasn't trying to be like a Dad," Ashley recalled. "But like a friend."

"It is hard to tell what was going through David's mind when he married Stacey," Orange said. "He was probably one of those men who just couldn't stand to be alone. He would hold his step-daughters at arm's length but deep down it appears that he wanted their affection. He just didn't know how to reciprocate it."

MORE MARRIAGE TROUBLE

While David appeared to be building bridges with the girls, the gap between he and his wife was widening. They would fight on a regular basis until they had a huge argument on their anniversary weekend. David wanted to go away while Stacey had other plans.

She would claim they fought throughout the day and that David went to his bedroom and locked himself in. She then sent both of her daughters to go stay with friends while she went off by herself to leave David alone.

David didn't arrive at his workplace the next day and Stacey "thought something was wrong." She called the sheriff's department and told them that he had locked himself in the bedroom. He wasn't responding to her knocks at the door nor was he responding to her texts. She told authorities that he was "depressed" and "maybe suicidal."

Sheriffs arrived and kicked in the door of the bedroom only to find David lying dead in a pool of vomit.

Near his body was a container of anti-freeze and a half-empty glass of the green liquid.

"He's not dead," Stacey screamed as she saw his prone body. "He's not dead!"

Detectives would confiscate the evidence from the scene although it had the obvious look of a suicide.

With her husband declared dead, Stacey called her daughters on the phone.

"I have something bad to tell you," the crying mother said. "And I don't know how to tell you. 'Well, what?' David killed himself."

The coroner would state that David killed himself by drinking a lethal amount of the anti-freeze. But an alert investigator noticed a turkey baster in the garbage can outside the garage. He took the item as evidence and had it tested.

"Something didn't feel right to the investigators," Orange said. "Luckily one of them had a sixth sense about the situation. Something about Stacey seemed a bit off as did the so-called suicide itself. Men typically do not take the passive way out of drinking poison or sleeping pills. They most commonly commit suicide by blowing their brains out. David owned a shotgun. That remained untouched. Yet he chose to commit suicide by ingesting anti-freeze which would be a really painful way to go. Why suffer when you can have it over and done with a pull of the trigger."

The forensic analysis would reveal Stacey's fingerprints as the only ones on the glass on David's bedside table. They also discovered that the turkey baster at David's DNA at the tip.

"If the door was locked," Orange said. "Then how did the turkey baster end up in the garage with his DNA."

This evidence led them to believe that Stacey had "force fed" the anti-freeze to David who was too weak to fight back.

"She had drugged him asleep," Orange said. "If you near death or unconscious you are not going to notice someone dripping anti-freeze into your mouth."

Investigators began making inquiries among David's friends and family. They kept getting the same answer.

"David wouldn't commit suicide."

Authorities didn't play their hand just yet. They played dumb, allowing Stacey to believe she was in the clear. They wiretapped her house and listened in on her calls for any incriminating statements. They then set up cameras that monitored both her house and the graves of her husbands as Stacey had them buried side by side.

"You had Mike on the far left," Corbett said. "David on the far right. I said 'what's she doing, starting a collection up there?'"

"She had her name engraved on both of the headstones," Bree said. "It's kinda weird."

But Stacey would never visit the graveyard where her husbands were buried. She did call a friend but told the friend that she "didn't do any of it."

Investigators needed more proof and decided to have Michael's body exhumed. They ran tests on his body that would reveal that he had ingested the anti-freeze just like David.

Back at home, Stacey was oblivious to the investigation. She went about her days in a daze, ignoring her daughters.

"After David died," Ashley recalled. "It was just as before. She didn't want to do things with me and my sister."

COLLECTING CASH

Stacey would benefit from receiving David's estate. His own son felt shock and hurt when he find out he was left out of the will.

"Things had deteriorated between us after the divorce," David Jr said. "And it hurt."

It would later be revealed that Stacey had doctored David's will to exclude his son and give all proceeds of his estate to her. She had a friend who was a notary who later admitted to helping Stacey with forging the document.

Stacey would inherit the home and the air conditioning business which she quickly sold for a profit.

"There was so much sweat that went into that business," David Jr said. "My grandfather started that business. And she just threw it away."

Stacey would receive $200,000 free and clear.

KILLING ASHLEY

By September 2007, Stacey felt the noose tightening around her neck. She eventually found out about the police exhuming Michael's body and finding the lethal dose of anti-freeze that she administered. Then the sheriff's arrived at her door.

One of the sheriffs described Stacey as having the 'deer in the headlights' look as they approached. The normally cool and collected Stacey stammered during their interrogation and mistakenly referred to a news story wherein the wife had poisoned her husband using "anti-free".

One of the sheriffs noted that she used the word 'anti-free' as opposed to 'anti-freeze'. This would later prove to be a huge mistake on Stacey's part.

Stacey would return home and she desperately needed a way out. She needed someone to take the blame. A blood sacrifice.

Even it was her own daughter.

Police would arrive on Ashley's college campus (Bryant & Stratton) to question her about her father's death. It was Ashley's first day of school and they informed her that stepfather had been poisoned instead of having a heart attack.

Ashley became angry at the investigators. She was insulted that they would even think that her mother could kill her father.

"I didn't believe that she did it," Ashley said. "I never thought for a second that she would ever hurt anybody. They couldn't figure out why he killed himself. They were just trying to pin it on somebody else."

Ashley was in disbelief and called her mother. Stacey invited her home.

"You've been through enough," Stacey said. "Come home and let's get drunk."

Ashley agreed, still trusting her mother as her 'best friend.' She arrived home and Stacey gave her a 'nasty-tasting' drink. It was a mixture of Vodka and Sprite.

And unknown to Ashley, anti-freeze was added to the cocktail.

"Just keep stirring it," Stacey told her daughter who spat up the drink. "It has Sprite in it."

"All I remember was going to sleep at one o'clock on Thursday," Ashley recalled. "Then when I wake up it isn't Thursday anymore it's Friday."

Hours later, Ashley would be found in a coma-like state by her sister Bree. She screamed for her mother to call 911 before seeing a note beside Ashley.

"I found this note by Ashley's bed," Bree recalled. "And it said all of this stuff, 'Dear Mommy, I'm sorry. And it was typed. And I was like 'Oh my God, you have to see this.'"

Stacey knew exactly what was happening to her daughter. Yet she played the role of the distraught mother to the hilt.

"My daughter has taken some pills," Stacey choked back tears as she spoke to the dispatcher. "It sounds like there's something in her throat. Ashley. Oh my God. Oh my God. Oh my God."

Medics would rush to home and take Ashley to the hospital. They had discovered she had ingested a lethal dose of painkillers. Stacey had crushed pain medication pills and poured them in Ashley's drink, creating a lethal cocktail. Had the paramedics arrived only minutes later, Ashley would have been dead.

Stacey made sure that the "confession" letter made it to the hands of the paramedics. The typewritten letter was over a page long, single-spaced, with Ashley giving details and specifics as to why she killed both her father and stepfather. At the end of the confession, she pleads for her mother "to forgive her."

Stacey did not expect her daughter to make it through. To her surprise, her daughter was revived and quickly questioned by police.

"It was all blurry," Ashley said. "All I remember was a man in a red shirt yelling, 'What did you drink? What did you take? What did you write in that note?'"

"The last thing I remember was my Mom giving me a drink," Ashley said. "It was something she had never done before."

The police officer was adamant about asking Ashley if she wrote the suicide note.

"I didn't write any notes," Ashley said, appearing confused about the question.

Witnessing the entire exchange, Bree would be the one to break the news to Ashley.

Their mother had tried to kill her.

ARRESTED AT LAST

Authorities would spend over two years accumulating evidence against Stacey. In 2007, she would be arrested for degree murder in David's death and for attempting to murder Ashley as well as frame her for the killings of David and Michael.

Ashley would be brought to the stand and testify that she did not kill David or Michael. She also said that she did not type up the computer-generated "confession" letter where she revealed that she killed both men. Stacey made a mistake in that she had prepared numerous drafts of Ashley's "confession" later on her computer. The drafts had timestamps and had been written while Ashley was away at college, proving that she could not have written the letters.

There was also repeated use of the word "anti-free" throughout the letter. This phrasing echoed what she had said during her interrogation with police.

Mounting further evidence, prosecuting attorneys argued that David's "suicide" didn't make any sense because his fingerprints were not on the glass of anti-freeze they found by his side. They stated that he had been force-fed the poison through the turkey baster. Stacey argued otherwise, saying that David got the idea after watching a documentary on Lynn Turner, a woman who would murder her lovers by using the poison.

"He was depressed lot," Stacey said. "The business wasn't going well."

THE DEFENSE

Stacey's defense team began attacking Ashley. They wanted to prove that she was someone capable of murder, even at age eleven.

They began documenting how Michael showed favoritism to Bree and that Ashley killed him out of jealousy. Belaboring the point, they said that Ashley never got along with her stepfather David and killed him out of jealousy as well.

Stacey would then be called to the stand. She stated that she thought Ashley was mentally ill. The prosecuting team then went to work on Stacey, shouting out their questions in an accusatory manner. They asked why if Ashley was mentally ill she had not one shred of medical history to corroborate that allegation.

Then came the coup de grace. The prosecution team revealed to the jury that it was Stacey's fingerprints alone on the "confession" letter and not Ashley's. They had wiretapped the home and stated that there were 'typing sounds' throughout the day.

The sounds of Stacey typing up the fake 'confession' letter.

The jury deliberated for only two days before pronouncing Stacey guilty on February 5th, 2009 of second-degree murder in the death of David and attempted murder for overdosing Ashley with drugs and Vodka

The judge ordered her to serve a maximum of 25 years to life for the murder of David and another 25 for the attempt to kill Ashley. An additional 1 to 4 years was added for forging David's will.

Ashley still retained mixed feelings about her mother as it all came as a shock to her.

"I never knew what hate was until now," Ashley said. "Even though I do hate her, I still love her at the same time. That bothers me, it is so confusing. How can you hate someone and love them at the same time? I just wish that she would say sorry for everything she did, including all the lies. As horrible as it makes me feel, this is goodbye mom. As hard as you tried, I survived and I will survive because now I'm surrounded by people that love me. I'm going to do good things in this world despite making me in every sense of the word an orphan."

RANTINGS OF A SOCIOPATH

Stacey would be admitted into the Bedford Hills Correctional Facility for Women in Bedford Hills, New York.

Stacey would continue to place guilt on her daughter, Ashley. "She brought this on," Stacey said. "Bree was an innocent victim in all of this. I lost her, I lost my husbands."

"I was happy that they said she was guilty," Bree said. "Because we all know that she's guilty."

Ashley would be haunted by her mother's betrayal forever.

"I would have done anything for her," Ashley said. "But she tried to kill me instead."

DEATH

Stacey would be found dead in her cell on June 11th, 2016. Her cause of death remains under investigation.

JUDY BUENOANO

50

Judy Buenoano loved men. But she loved killing them more.

In 1971, she murdered her husband James and nine years later she would kill her own son, Michael. In 1983, she would attempt but fail to kill her boyfriend, John Gentry. She is also believed to have been responsible for the death of Bobby Joe Morris (another boyfriend) in 1978. She was never convicted of the Morris crime, however, as by the time the authorities had connected the dots she was sentenced to death for the murder of her first husband.

But the suspicions didn't stop with the Morris death. Buenoano is also suspected of killing a man in 1974 and in 1980, another boyfriend would die under suspicious circumstances.

Buenoano would become the first woman executed in Florida since 1848 and only the third woman executed since capital punishment had been reinstated in 1976.

She would be sent to the electric chair in 1998. Her last words were that she wanted to be remembered as a "good mother."

Instead, she would go down as one of the most sadistic female serial killers in American history.

This is her story.

EARLY LIFE

Judy was born Judias Welty in Quanah, Texas on April 4th, 1943. Her father was a day laborer at a local farm. Judy would talk about her mother being a full-blooded member of the Mesquite Apache tribe but little did she know that a "Mesquite Apache" tribe didn't exist.

Her mother would die of tuberculosis when Judy was only two years old. She and her baby brother Robert would be sent to live with their grandparents while their two older siblings would be put up for adoption.

"When Judy's mother died," forensic psychologist Paula Orange said. "It sent Judy's life into a tailspin. This is one of those 'Butterfly Effect' scenarios. A tragic circumstance that occurred early in a child's life that led to her perpetuating pain on everyone else for the rest of her own adult life."

She would eventually leave her grandparents and join her father in Roswell, New Mexico. He had remarried and Judy would claim that both he and her new stepmother would beat, starve, and burn her with cigarettes.

They made her a "house slave", forcing her to do chores around the house at their bidding. Judy would finally act out at the age of fourteen as she would burn two of her step brothers with hot grease. Not stopping there, she attacked both her father and step-mom with fists flying.

Police would be called and Judy would be jailed for over two months. After she served her jail time, the judge gave Judy a choice, either return home or go to reform school. She opted for the latter and was sent to Foothills High School. She would remain there until 1959 when she would graduate at the age of sixteen.

She held her entire family in contempt, particularly her younger brother Robert.

"I wouldn't spit down his throat if his guts were on fire," Judy once said when asked about her brother.

CHANGING IDENTITY

Judy returned to Roswell but changed her name to "Anna Schultz". She found work as a nurse aide and would give birth to a baby boy out of wedlock, Michael Schultz on March 30, 1961. Judy would remain silent on the identity of the baby's father but people believed that Judy was having an affair with a pilot from the nearby air force base.

In 1963, the twenty-two-year-old Judy would marry James Goodyear. Goodyear was twenty-nine years old and serving as a sergeant in the United States Air Force.

They would have their first child together, James Jr, four years later. James would celebrate the event by legally adopting Michael. Daughter

Kimberly would come a year later as the family would move to Orlando, Florida.

Judy would then open her own business, starting the Conway Acres Child Care Center in Orlando. She listed James as the co-owner even though he was during a one-year tour in the Vietnam War. After returning home, he only had three months of downtime before he was admitted to the U.S. Naval Hospital in Orlando, complaining from symptoms staff physicians never quite identified. He would die on September 15, 1971.

Goodyear was only thirty-seven years old at the time of death and authorities believed he died due to natural causes.

"He came home from Vietnam ill and he never got well," Judy said. ``It had nothing to do with me. I was not in Vietnam."

"Crazy that Goodyear was able to survive the horrors of Vietnam but not Judy Buenoano," Orange said. "He had no idea he was married to a sociopath. She had no respect for the fact that he had just put himself on the line for her and the country. All she saw were dollar signs."

Judy poisoned James with arsenic and waited almost a week after his death before cashing in his three life insurance policies. A few months later, an "accidental fire" burned down their Orlando home. Judy would receive another $90,000 in fire insurance.

She lost her husband and her home. But her purse was never fatter.

NO GRIEVING WIDOWS ALLOWED

Judy would waste no time finding another man. Despite having three kids in tow, she would find a new love in Bobby Joe Morris when she moved her family to Pensacola.

It was business as usual for Judy as she had a fat bank account courtesy of James Goodyear and a new beau in Bobby Joe. Eldest son Michael, however, was not doing well in school. He scored on the low end on IQ tests and was a behavioral problem. Judy would get him evaluated at a state hospital in 1974 and then sent Michael out to foster care where he would also receive psychiatric treatment.

Judy's new home would suffer another "accidental fire" and she collected money from the insurance. She then took Michael out of foster care and moved to Trinidad, Colorado with Bobby Joe and the rest of her children. Judy then changed her name from "Anna Schultz" to "Judias Morris".

FOUR YEARS MAX

Judy would date Bobby Joe for four years before deciding it was time to cut him loose.

Bobby Joe would start to suffer from the same mysterious illness as James Goodyear did years earlier as he complained of dizziness and vomiting. He would be admitted to San Rafael Hospital on January 4, 1978, but doctors would not be able to pinpoint what was wrong with him. He would be sent home to Judy's care two weeks later. Two days later, however, he would would pitch face-first into his dinner plate, unconscious. He would be rushed to the hospital, but Judy knew that her "medicine" had taken effect.

Five days later, Bobby Joe Morris would be dead. Doctors would chalk up his death to cardiac arrest and metabolic acidosis.

Judy would wait, just like she did after she killed James, before cashing in on Bobby Joe's life insurance.

Authorities were none the wiser.

But Bobby Joe's family suspected something fishy was going on. Back in 1974, Judy and Bobby Joe had been visiting Brewton, Alabama when a man from Florida was found dead in a motel room in that town. Police would find the man in the room after receiving an anonymous call. He was shot in the chest with a .22-caliber weapon and his throat was cut open.

Judy's connection to the crime? Bobby Joe's mother had overheard Judy telling her son about the murder.

"The sonofabitch shouldn't have come up here in the first place," Judy said. "If he came up here he was gonna die."

Bobby Joe had told his mother about the crime on his deathbed. She thought the confession could be attributed to his delirium, but Bobby Joe told her too many specifics to ignore.

"We should never had done that terrible thing," Bobby Joe mumbled to his mother. "Never should have done that to him."

She tipped off police but they would not be able to find any fingerprints inside the room and no bullet was recovered from the corpse. The case remained unsolved.

WHAT'S ONE MORE SURNAME?

On May 3rd, 1978, Judy would change her name again. This go around, she would change her last name to Buenoano, which in Spanish meant "good year." She stated that she meant it as a tribute to her husband James Goodyear and her Apache mother.

Things continued to go bad with Michael as he dropped out of high school in the tenth grade. With limited employment opportunities, he would join the army in June of 1979 and get assigned to Ft. Benning in Georgia after basic training. When he was on his way to his new post, he visited Judy in Pensacola.

Judy greeted her son with open arms. Then she began poisoning him.

By the time he reached Ft. Benning, he felt sick. Army physicians would find seven times the normal level of arsenic in his body.

They could do little to reverse the damage done. Six weeks after his arrival, the muscles in his arms and legs and deteriorated to the point where he was a paraplegic.

"Michael had no use of his legs," Orange said. "And he could not move his arms past his elbow. Again, Judy was a sociopath. It is unfathomable for a normal human being, a mother, to do this to her own child. Yet she did it to Michael. He was always an inconvenience to her but now that he had military insurance he could become an asset in death."

Judy would give Michael the short shrift while favoring James and Kimberly. Michael and James didn't get along well as clearly their mother favored the latter. Judy would hide Michael when people came over because she was ashamed of him. She would have a neighbor named Constance Lang watch over him when visitors arrived.

"Michael didn't fit the picture Judy wanted to present to the world," Orange said. "She wanted to be looked at like a woman of high status. She drove a Corvette and owned her own business. Michael was a slow-thinking kid. She didn't want anyone to see that."

The army didn't investigate the reasons behind Michael's inordinate levels of arsenic. Instead, they set him up with leg braces and a prosthetic device on one of his arms.

He would be discharged from active duty because of the medical disability.

But his mother saw dollar signs.

The day after his return home, Judy wasted no time. She organized a fishing trip with Michael, James, and daughter Kimberly. They would leave Kimberly ashore at the East River bridge while they went into the water with a two-seat canoe. A small folding lawn chair had been placed in the middle of the canoe for Michael who had was outfitted with a leg brace, a fishing reel, and a ski belt.

James would state that had fished for about two hours when they were reaching shore when a "snake fell into the canoe." He said that everyone panicked as the snake slithered around. The canoe hit a log and capsized.

James would claim to have been knocked out by the impact and would remember nothing until he came to inside an ambulance.

He would tell this version to the court but when he was talking to Army investigators, he made no mention of a snake.

"There is conjecture as to how much James was involved or much did he know," Orange said. "The statement given to the army investigators is different from what he would state later in court. The statement given to the army was a written statement and the handwriting didn't seem to match his own."

A man named Ricky Hicks saw the overturned canoe, an ice chest, and a plastic bag in the river. He also saw Judy and James.

"I lost the other boy," Judy said as Ricky approached them on the shore. "A snake had gotten into the canoe and I tried to hold the snake down with a paddle."

"Where is he?"

"It's no use," Judy said, waving him off.

Hicks said Judy appeared to be concerned about James then asked him for a beer. He then drove Judy's car to a nearby phone and called the county rescue squad.

The rescue team arrived and began looking for the missing Michael.

The canoe had not moved as there was barely a current. They would find Michael's body one-quarter of a mile upriver where the canoe had been rescued. The rescuers stated that it should not have been a problem to swim upstream, suggesting that Michael could have been saved.

Judy initially said that Michael had a life jacket on but later recanted and said that it was a ski belt.

There was no ski belt on Michael when he was found.

Judy would later state that after the canoe capsized, she saw James lying face down in the water. She swam over and cleared his air passage to resuscitate him. She looked around for Michael then was picked up by Ricky Hicks.

"Michael disappeared under water," Judy said. "I went to rescue James. I almost lost both of my sons that day. Mothers just don't murder their children. If I'd have lost both of them, I don't know what I would have done. They would have had to put me in a mental institution."

"Kimberly's boyfriend would later testify that Judy had killed Michael for the insurance money," Orange said. "The children knew about their mother but she had clearly brainwashed them into silence. She provided for them, she fed them. She knew what was best."

Telling the police that she was a "clinical physician", they bought her story of the boat capsizing. The army investigators did not buy her account. Not having any evidence, however, they would eventually pay her Michael's military life insurance ($20,000). Investigators got suspicious, however, when they found out that two civilian life policies were taken out on Michael. The applications on both policies look to have been forged.

Judy's former sister-in-law, Peggy Goeller, would call to inquire how she was doing. She would make no mention of Michael's death during her first call but on a second call she told Peggy that Michael had died "during Army maneuvers".

MOVING ON

Judy would demonstrate very little grief over Michael's death and she would not be charged with his murder. Foremost on her mind was finding another man and another big check.

She opened a beauty salon in Gulf Breeze and found her next mark: businessman John Gentry.

Gentry was more well-heeled than her previous conquests so Judy put on airs for his sake. She told him that she had Ph.D.'s in biochemistry and psychology and was the former head of nursing at West Florida Hospital.

Gentry believed her story and decided to spoil his blue-blooded girlfriend expensive gifts, vacations and the finest cuisine all in the name of courtship.

Pushing the envelope, Judy would encourage John to provide life insurance for both them both. She then secretly boosted Gentry's coverage from $50,000 to $500,000 without him knowing.

Two months later, Judy began giving Gentry "vitamin pills".

"Come on," she said, placing two pills into Gentry's palm.

"What are you, my mother?" Gentry asked.

"Well, God forbid I want to see you healthy," Judy slid the cup of water toward her prey.

Gentry would then complain of dizziness and later begin vomiting after his daily dose of Judy's "vitamins."

He would admit himself into the hospital and noticed that his symptoms disappeared when he stopped taking the vitamins.

Still smitten by Judy, he did not suspect her of wrongdoing. Instead, he took her vitamins and hid them in his briefcase.

One night, however, Judy sat him down for a special dinner. She had a very special announcement.

"I'm pregnant," she said, smiling in triumph.

"Finally," Gentry said. He told Judy that they should celebrate. She told him to go to the liquor store for an expensive bottle of champagne.

"Be right back," he said, kissing her with excitement.

Running out the door, Gentry got into his car and a bomb exploded with he turned the ignition key.

Amazingly, Gentry survived the blast as trauma surgeons saved his life.

"Judy really overplayed her hand with the explosion in the car," Orange said. "Really it speaks to her level of dedication and ingenuity. Who knows where she got the idea, maybe watching the Godfather. But the police found the dynamite residue inside Gentry's car. They decided to look no further than to Judy herself."

Their interrogation and research would unearth lie after lie. They found out about the $450,000 increase in Gentry's life insurance.

Gentry himself thought the insurance had been canceled. He was shocked to learn that she had increased the payout and was paying his premiums out of her own pocket. The police didn't spare him any quarter. They would him that she was not a real doctor and that she couldn't get pregnant.

"What?" Gentry muttered, completely flabbergasted.

Judy had been sterilized seven years earlier.

Gentry couldn't believe his ears. Police would go on to say that she had booked tickets for a world cruise for herself and her children...leaving Gentry out. They discovered that Judy had been telling her friends that Gentry was suffering from a "terminal illness."

The only "terminal illness" Gentry had was Judy Buenoano.

Now fully convinced, Gentry would reach into his briefcase and give police the "vitamin pills" that Judy had been giving him.

"Judy was emptying the vitamin casing and filling it with formaldehyde and a little arsenic," Orange said. "Over time, this would have been lethal."

The state attorney would refuse to charge Judy as they wanted an air tight case in order to prosecute. Knowing that they had their killer, officers, and federal agents searched Judy's home in Gulf Breeze, obtaining wire and tape from her bedroom that looked to match the same wire/tape they found on the bomb in Gentry's car.

They would search her son James' room, finding marijuana and a sawed-off shotgun. He would be jailed him for possession of drugs and an illegal weapon.

"Again, this is a strange mistake on Judy's part," Orange said. "She was meticulous and a good liar. Why she didn't remove any and all evidence from her home is a head-scratcher. She had gotten sloppy because she had gotten away with so many crimes before without so much as a slap on the wrist. She thought she was above the law, got careless and left incriminating evidence behind."

Judy would then be arrested at her beauty salon and charged with attempted murder. It took a month of police work, but authorities would trace the source of the dynamite used in the bomb, linking the Alabama buyer to Judy via phone records which showed numerous long-distance calls from her home.

Judy would pay bail but authorities would not let up. Five months later, she would be indicted for first-degree murder in the death of her son Michael, with an additional count of grand theft for the insurance scam.

Feeling the noose around her neck, Judy would fake a seizure and wind up in Santa Rosa Hospital.

Authorities then exhumed the bodies of the men they believed she killed. Bobby Joe Morris was exhumed with arsenic found in his remains. Identical results were obtained with the exhumation of James Goodyear, in the following month.

Connecting the dots, police obtained a court order to exhume the bodies of all the men that had died while associated with Judy; son Michael, husband James Goodyear, and boyfriend Bobby Joe Morris.

Arsenic would be found in all of the bodies.

"There was enough arsenic in him (Goodyear) to kill twelve people," Detective Ted Chamberlain said. "So he was loaded. I mean that boy was loaded with it when he went down."

OPEN AND SHUT CASE

In 1984, Judy would be convicted of the murders of Michael and attempted murder of Gentry. In a separate trial in 1985, she would be convicted of the murder of James Goodyear in which she would ultimately receive the death sentence.

Judy would be imprisoned in the Florida Department of Corrections Broward Correctional Institution death row for women.

HER FINAL HOURS

Judy would spend her last day watching a hunting and fishing show, eating chocolates, and talking about old times with her children and cousin Jeanne Eaton. She would read a suspense novel called "Remember Me" and her last meal with be steamed broccoli, asparagus, strawberries and hot tea.

Judy's impending execution did not receive the same media attention as Karla Faye Tucker whose was executed only a month earlier. Her execution was opposed by the Pope and Jesse Jackson.

'"She may not have been as photogenic, as young or as pretty as Karla, but she was just as good a Christian," Eaton said.

"Judy obviously had her enablers within her family," Orange said. "How could she be 'just as good a Christian' if she is poisoning people, blowing them up and the 'Christian' she is being compared to is ice-picking people to death. People say the strangest things."

But Judy herself was bitter that no one paid much attention to her presence on death row, particularly the fact that she was a woman.

``Karla was a young female, very attractive and she had become a Christian in prison," Judy said. ``We all prayed that she would be granted a stay of execution and clemency because we felt that she was a different person and she deserved a chance. Possibly, I am a different person. But I was a Christian when I came here. I was a devout Catholic. I've not changed in that."

"It was a bit of a curiosity as to why the media was so charged to prevent the execution of Karla Faye Tucker and paid little heed to Buenoano," Orange said. "Tucker's killings were ferocious and sadistic while Buenoano's killings could be seen as passive. But what drew people to Tucker was her physical appearance and demeanor. She came across as a sweet, reformed choir girl at the end. She had a charming smile and a soft voice. Buenoano, on the other hand, looked sinister. She had squinty eyes, high cheekbones and a snarling, Southern drawl. Her body language and demeanor screamed hostile."

Judy would enter the death chamber with several guards by her side. They strapped her into the large oak chair, placing leather straps over her waist, wrists, chest, and legs.

They fitted the calf and headpiece electrodes last, inserting a wet sponge in between to reduce the burning of Judy's skin.

"Do you have a final statement?" the warden asked.

"No, sir," Judy closed her eyes tight.

The witnesses on the other side of the glass partition watched in silence.

Judy did not look at them as a leather mask was placed over her face.

The warden nodded his head and the switch was pulled.

Steam wafted up from her right leg as her body jolted for thirty-eight seconds. Her hands balled into fists, white knuckling from the shock as smoke rose from her feet to the ceiling.

Then Judy went limp. She would be pronounced dead at 7:08 a.m., March 30th, 1998.

The date was her son Michael's 37th birthday.

HUSBAND KILLER JANE DOROTIK

ANNA MICHAELS

Murder at the Charisma Ranch

Robert Dorotik was born in 1945, two years before his future wife Jane Marguerite Colvey. It would be 23 years before they would meet and fall in love. They married on April 4, 1970 in Los Angeles California.

Two years later Nicholas was born, another son Alexander would follow shortly after that and by January 16, 1976 their family would be complete with the birth of their daughter Claire Elizabeth.

Robert was an Engineer and Jane was a Health care professional as well as a successful business woman. She made a six figure salary from her 9-5 job alone, and the horse ranch she ran with her daughter was starting to bring in money too.

Robert and Jane would have more than one argument over the money Jane and their daughter Claire spent on Charisma Ranch. He quit his job as an engineer to support Jane's endeavor of raising and training horses. Bob started a business making horse jumps, but by 2000 his business was in trouble. One of the last arguments Jane and Bob had was when Jane and Claire told him they found another horse that would be perfect for the ranch. Robert complained they didn't need any more horses. This infuriated Jane and she told him in no uncertain terms that it was her money and she would spend it how she wanted, she didn't need his permission.

On the afternoon of February 13, 2000 Jane got ready to go down to tend to the horses. Bob was dressing in his jogging clothes and told Jane he was going to go for a run. Bob had been a long distance runner for years. Jane had an injury that prevented her from participating. Jane asked her husband to stoke the fire before he left and she went to the barn.

Mrs. Dorotik returned to the house a couple hours later and Bob was nowhere to be found. She waited a while longer and began looking for him. There were others including neighbors and sons Nick and Alex. Becoming increasingly worried about her husband Jane called the police and told them that he had not come home after his run. A search was organized by the police and in the early morning hours of February 14, 2000 Police found Robert's battered, bloodied body by the side of the road about three miles from home. Police immediately suspected Jane.

Robert Dorotik had died from blunt force trauma and strangulation. He had several injuries to the face and the back of the head (an expert testified the wounds were consistent with a hammer). There were defensive wounds on his hands. He was still wearing his jogging clothes although according to the detectives his shoes were tied in an odd manner. The rope used to strangle him was still around his neck and had made a laceration on his throat.

They did not find blood at the scene that would have been consistent with it being the murder site. Robert had been killed somewhere else and moved here. They found the tire tracks and shoe prints. Jane could not be linked to any of the shoe prints, only the tire tracks. However, hers were not the only tire tracks there, the others were not linked to anyone.

The evidence from the beginning seemed to point at Jane Dorotik as the killer. At the scene where they found the body there were tire tracks that matched the three different treads on her truck. At the residence there was a massive amount of blood that had been cleaned at. Jane claims that the blood was from a nosebleed Robert had and cleaned up. Between the box springs and mattress there was a towel soaked with blood. In a bag in the master bedroom they found a syringe with a horse tranquilizer in it and Jane's fingerprint in Bob's blood was found on it. She was arrested before the blood analysis could even be returned.

Around the room investigators found impact blood spatter patterns as well as drip, transfer and cast off. In one of the closets in the house they found a steam carpet shampooer and a significant amount of cleaning supplies. Bob's blood was found on the cap, handle and nozzle of one of the bottles.

Blood stains consistent with Robert's were found in the bed of the truck Jane, Claire and the ranch hands used around the ranch. They found no blood spatter on his shoes or shirt, but did find some blood on his boxers. One of the two hands never showed up for work the day after Bob's death.

Jane was booked into San Diego County Jail and with the help of family made bail.

Jane's daughter Claire was incriminated in the murder, that she was actually the one that killed Robert, her own father. It was well known that father and daughter had a stormy relationship, and at times became volatile. It was never revealed why the two seemed to hate each other, but Claire even wrote a scathing letter to her father about a "betrayal of trust."

Jane's defense team Kerry Steigerwalt and Cole Casey now had to figure out how to defend their 55 year old client. What they decided on wasn't the most unusual way to do it and it and many other attorneys had done in numerous courtrooms around the country. They deliberately brought Claire up as a suspect. By showing that another person 'could' have committed the murder there is a chance that it will raise enough of a doubt in a jury's mind for them to bring back an acquittal instead of a guilty verdict. This is what the attorney's for Jane were doing, trying to raise a reasonable doubt. This strategy would ultimately tear the family apart. In a letter written three years after her conviction Jane would call her attorney 'ego driven' and the implicating of her daughter a 'seriously flawed defense strategy.'

Prosecutor Bonnie Howard-Regan was convinced that Jane killed her husband to keep from having to pay him spousal support. It seemed there was an impending divorce on the horizon for Bob and Jane. They had separated in 1997 but talked it out and decided to keep their money separate and got back together.

Their own sons commented that their parents' marriage wasn't the most loving and at times their fights became very heated. But is this a motive for murder? Perhaps not just the fights, maybe it was the fact that if the two divorced Jane would have to pay Robert up to 40% of her annual income. This would be upwards of 50,000 dollars a year. Jane was incensed when a divorce attorney had told her that. That is a huge motive for murder in the eyes of the law. There was also a $250,000 life insurance policy on both Bob and Jane. She was forthcoming with the detectives about this during the investigation. If she had to pay that much out in spousal support she wouldn't be able to keep the horse ranch, and it seemed that was all she cared about.

Jane's trial would begin in May of 2001 a little over a year after her husband was murdered. Jane had pled not guilty and was making passionate pleas to the public declaring her innocence. Though her daughter and sister also claimed that Jane was innocent of this heinous crime, Claire, Bonnie Long and a ranch hand all invoked their Fifth Amendment right against self-incrimination. Steigerwalt brought up the fact that Claire's alibi was never confirmed. Had the Sheriff's Department zeroed in on Jane in a hasty attempt to close the case?

On June 9, 2001 the case of Jane Dorotik v The State of California went to the jury for deliberation. After the third day both the defense and the prosecution were starting to worry. Maybe they hadn't presented their case as well as they'd thought. Maybe they didn't explain things in an easy to understand way. In the end however, it wasn't that the jury had a problem understanding what they saw and heard during the trial. They were just being diligent, making sure every juror understood what the evidence was and how it fit in the scheme of things. In fact, they had a unanimous decision on the first vote...guilty on the charge of first degree murder.

Judge Joan Weber said that there was "an overwhelming amount of circumstantial evidence" and when Jane's attorney filed for a new trial it was denied. New witnesses had come forward and Steigerwalt asked that the case be reopened to the jury could hear what they had to say. She denied his request. Weber also asked, "How could you have your husband's blood on your hands if you had nothing to do with his death?" The Judge Weber was referring to the syringe with Janes fingerprint on it. It was an integral piece of evidence in the case.

Without a new trial in San Diego County, the next step is Court Of Appeal Of California, Fourth Appellate District, Division One.

The Court of Appeals works differently than the Trial Court. It is not a place for a new trial or a retrial. They won't look at new evidence or hear from new witnesses. It is strictly for trying to overturn the lower court's decision. If this happens then the Trial Court would be made to do one of several different actions in the case. One would be a whole new trial, which in Jane's case is what her attorney would want to happen. Or perhaps the Appellate Court would order Trial Court to look at additional evidence and/or revisit the facts in the case.

Either of these would be a win for Jane and her defense team. However, before these could happen her attorney would have to show that there was an error in the trial procedure or in how Weber interpreted the law.

This all starts with a Notice to Appeal, and then a brief has to be filed. In many cases appeals are decided based solely on this brief. Other times there will oral arguments before anything is decided.

Janes appeal was filed on November 18, 2003. She is asserting that Judge Weber should have included in the instructions to the jury the lessor charge of voluntary manslaughter because the state didn't present evidence that there was premeditation and aforethought to constitute first degree murder. She was denied.

On June 12, 2009 Jane filed another appeal. There were three key facts in this appeal. In the first one she claims 'ineffective assistance of counsel'. Jane claimed that her defense team didn't represent her properly. They didn't do any investigation of their own.

Second, she believed that not letting the jury hear from the new witnesses and not doing DNA testing jeopardized her case. The rope used to strangle Robert was never test for DNA, claiming that epithelia's of the real killer would have been found.

Third, there were procedural mistakes because of the delayed discovery and her actual innocence.

The defense was not allowed to present evidence that the State's expert witness had many mistakes in other cases by using 'faulty methodology'. The jury was not allowed to hear from an eyewitness.

The Appellate Court denied her, again.

The San Diego Union-Tribune reported on November 22, 2015 that a Judge has determined Jane be allowed to have the DNA in her case tested. The rope used to strangle Bob, the fingernail scrapings, and a piece of hair found around the victim's finger all be tested.

Jane still proclaims her innocence and said the ranch hand that didn't show up for work the day after the murder should be considered. He drives a black pick-up, and his tire tracks were also found at the scene. She also reiterated that the man owed the Dorotik's money.

Jane filed her first appeal on November 18, 2003. The Appellate court upheld the lower court's decision. Then Jane, known also as the petitioner filed Habeas petition on April 4, 2006 in the State Superior Court. Next was a Habeas Petition in the Appellate Court on January 3, 2006. And again Jane filed with the State Supreme Court on November 20, 2006. All appeals and motions to this point had been denied or affirmed the lower court's decision.

On June 1, 2007 Jane would file a Petition for Writ of Habeas Corpus, a Motion to appoint counsel, a Motion for Leave to Proceed in Forma Pauperis and a request for DNA testing. This too was denied or dismissed.

In July of 2007 Jane managed to get the money for filing fees and Magistrate Judge Porter ordered the case be reopened on July 9, 2007.

In the appeal for ineffectual assistance of counsel the superior court "denied the claims on the merits in a written order but only addressed the first two claims. On appeal the Appellate Court did the same thing.

Jane contends that council should have done independent testing of the forensic evidence that the prosecution would be presenting at trial and that there was other available evidence that he could have taken advantage of but didn't. Jane contends that had he done so the findings would have weakened the prosecution's case.

Another point the petitioner brought up is that her counsel didn't call her as a witness in her own defense.

Petitioner wanted a medical professional called as an expert witness to testify as to the medical impossibility that she could have perpetrated the murder due to an injury from an accident years earlier. That she would not have had the strength to do what the prosecution says she did.

Counsel for the defense did not object when a detective testified that he thought she was the killer. He could have also asked for a mistrial also.

He didn't insist on DNA testing prior to the start of the trial, armed with the results of the tests, petitioner is sure that it would have pointed to the real killer or killers.

Petitioner believes that her counsel should have brought up different scenarios that could have explained away the circumstantial evidence brought up at trial.

That he could have provided innocent theories for the incriminating evidence.

He didn't show that police didn't follow any leads, including eyewitnesses that came forward in the early stages of the investigation; they made up their mind that she was guilty. Therefore they didn't look for the real killer/killers.

Jane contends that her counsel could have done their own investigation and found the witnesses that were not heard at trial. Instead he made the leap to blaming Claire Dorotik as a defense.

And finally, follow through on the promises counsel made to the jury about what the evidence would show, and not make a comment to the affect that Jane was guilty.

If none of these ten points were true but the last one, would that fact that her own defense counsel made a comment that directly or indirectly told the jury he thought she was guilty should have been grounds for a mistrial and perhaps proceedings started to disbar her attorney.

The points brought up in Jane's eyes caused her to be wrongly convicted for the murder of her husband.

The forensic evidence in many parts does not support the prosecution's theory. Think about the "blood" found on the wall that supposedly dripped down from the master bedroom upstairs. The man who sold /rented the property to the Dorotik's knew of a water leak. Rain water would get in the track of the sliding door and seep down the wall of the stairs leading to the bedroom. There was Bob's DNA there, but was it from blood? Walking shirtless up the stairs and rubbing his sweaty arm on the wall could leave his DNA, it was not said that it was blood.

Post-conviction reports showed that there was way less blood present than would have been if the State's expert witness, Merrit, were correct. McDonell who did the post-conviction report says the fatal blow probably occurred outside the bedroom. But at the same time doesn't accept the idea that Bob was killed where he was found or that he was killed somewhere else, body dumped where it was found and the blood evidence planted.

McDonell also said that the blood on the mattress could have easily been caused by a bloody nose. That being said it still doesn't explain the different blood stain patterns found throughout the room. Those where found on the pillow, nightstand, walls, bedspread and the window. Those he said cannot be explained away by a nosebleed.

The post-conviction report says that Merrit's testimony was wrong inasmuch as there was not enough blood soaked in to support his idea that Bob remained on the mattress for a long time after the attack.

McDonell concurs with petitioner that the blood around the pot-belly stove could very well have been from the nosebleed. Petitioner wants further testing to find out if it even had anything to do with the murder at all.

The bloody thumb print on the syringe was due to Bob helping Jane with a vet procedure. There was a horse tranquilizer inside the syringe and Jane's thumbprint in Bob's blood on it. This was admitted into evidence? Why, it's said to be a 'key piece' of evidence in the prosecution's case. Petitioner's counsel didn't object? Per Bob's toxicology report there was no drugs in his system. How did they tie it into the murder?

The truck, tire tracks and shoe prints. There was much to do about the tire tracks at the scene where Bob's body was found. There were actually two sets, one belonging to the family truck, the one that everyone including the farm hands had access to. But there was another set, never identified. The shoe prints found also at the scene couldn't be attributed to Jane either. Both sets were too big. The tracks that showed Jane's truck had backed up at the spot where the body was found can easily be explained as well. Bob used the truck to measure jogging routes. If he were to come to the exact length he wanted, he would have just turned around at that spot, hence the backup tracks.

A cursory search of the house was done the evening that Jane reported Bob missing. Police and Police dogs were all in the house including the master bedroom. They didn't find any blood.

Jane was in an accident in 1983 and had a severe injury to a hip which had to be put back together with metal and screws. The prosecution says that Jane would have bludgeoned her husband, then carried him down the stairs from the bedroom, through the house, across a 60' porch and lifted him into the back of a full sized Ford

F250. Defense counsel should have brought up the fact that his client couldn't have done any of that. The Appellate court says that her sons saw her pulling irrigation pipes around the ranch that weighed about 75 lbs. pulling on 75lbs of something is different than lifting 147 lbs of dead weight.

Detective Richard Empson when questioned about the rope used to strangle Robert Dorotik and why it wasn't tested for DNA said the "criminologists in his office discouraged testing it because too many people had handled it." When pressed about the possibility of DNA on it that could have belonged to Claire or the ranch hand Leonel Morales or someone else and lead to the real killer, what then? Empson continued, "I believe I know who killed Bob Dorotik, that's why I arrested Jane Dorotik." Personal opinions are not supposed to be brought in to testimony, especially from an officer of the court. Did Jane's counsel object to this? Did it prejudice the jury against the petitioner? It could be said that it inflamed the jury. Most jurors will believe a law enforcement officer over anyone else. Even if the comment was objected to and stricken from the record the juror's still heard it and no matter if they are told to disregard it, it will still be in their mind.

There are so many points that Jane brought up on each one of her appeals. And each and every one of them were dismissed by the Courts. Many of Jane's friends and family still believe that Jane is innocent and should at least get a new trial so all of the evidence can be heard and that maybe she can even testify in her own defense. Although her trial court attorney believed that doing so was not a good idea. Clearly he didn't believe his client was innocent of the crime.

In the findings of the Appellate Court they say that the petitioner didn't show how not having the jury hear that Merrit's methodology was flawed and that he had been wrong on other cases would not have changed the jury's verdict.

They stated that even though the petitioner believes that the prosecution purposefully did not test for DNA she cannot prove how it would have changed anything. Also added the testing would not have brought forth any exculpatory or impeaching evidence. Knowing that DNA has set wrongfully convicted people free by proving their innocence this statement seems wrong in its entirety. Jane would be in a Catch 22 scenario, she can't prove that by not testing there was an error in law and without being able to prove it would help her case they wouldn't allow the testing.

Jane says she's been through a living hell since being sent to Chowchilla's prison facility in central California. But she hasn't been wasting her time. Along with filing the above mentioned appeals she is fighting for her fellow prisoners who are over the age of 55.

Jane is appalled at how many women are incarcerated and how the number keeps growing every year. She was once a mental health professional and says that a large number of women in prison should be in a Mental Health facility.

According to Jane "Medical care is liken to a third world country." And "there are women dying in prison alone and unnoticed by prison staff.

What she is trying to get done is this, have more compassionate releases, the parole board has the authority to do this but won't. So a program is working its way through legislation in the state of California. "If The Risk Is Low, Let Them Go".

Jane isn't advocating opening the flood gates and letting these women head off to parts unknown. There are a certain set of criteria in place to make sure the risk is actually low.

First of all, they have to have served at least 50% of their sentence or seven years.

They can't have had any disciplinary actions in the past five years. In other words they have to be a model prisoner.

They cannot have any other felony convictions of their record and they must have a concrete, safe place to stay in the community

These are safeguards to keep reoffenders inside the prison walls. Jane is very passionate about this program. She has watched many of what she calls "Golden Girls" languishing with terminal illnesses for years, alone, not able to be with family because Chowchilla houses inmates from all over the state.

Many of the families just don't have the money or time to be able to travel to see their loved ones. And even the children have to be patted down before they can go in to see a relative, to possibly say a last goodbye.

Jane's alternative custody program has to clear through law makers and with the help of different advocates it's headed in the right direction thanks to Carol Lui a senator from California.

This is being heralded as a great program to help with overcrowding of the prisons in California, and if this comes about in a timely manner it could help Jane as well. She is now 68 years old.

HUSBAND KILLER SHEILA DAVALLOO

NATHAN NIXON

Sheila Davalloo

Sheila Davalloo is truly one of the most demented individuals of the past twenty years. Several serious crimes are still being added to her gruesome resume. She portrayed the persona of a pleasant, happy person. She hid dark secrets, however, as to who she really was. The main victim was simply caught in a position that she could never escape from. To understand the vicious crime that Sheila Davalloo committed, it is important to understand the background of who she was. The totality of this murder is one that is still being uncovered. The lasting effects on an entire group of people has truly been catastrophic.

Sheila Davalloo was born on May 11, 1969 in Iran. She and her family immigrated to the United States in the mid-1970s. Like many other immigrants of the time, her family settled in New York in the town of Yorktown Heights. She obtained a great education while in the United States. She excelled in her classes and graduated near the top of her class. She was one of the most committed students in her school during her time there. Her family had really instilled a strong sense of pride in learning and continued education. She went on to go to college at SUNY Stony Brook on Long Island. This was a great location for her as it allowed her to stay close to home. Her family had a close bond and desired to have a strong relationship with Sheila. She went on to earn a degree in biochemistry in four years of schooling. This is an advanced degree and requires great dedication. This speaks to the mind of Sheila Davalloo and her ability to think logically and on a higher level than most.

Just after graduating college, she went on to start her life according to the "American Dream". She married her first husband, Farid Moussavi, in the year after her graduation. Farid was a close family friend that the Davalloo family had known for many years. He was a business man who had established a strong reputation in the area. Their marriage, however, would not last long. It is well understood that Sheila was never in love with Farid. This marriage went back to the culture of the Middle East of the time of family approved marriage. This was more of a marriage to appease the wants of her family. Her next step would lead her to cross paths with her gruesome reality.

Sheila Davalloo attended graduate program classes New York Medical School. She desired to apply her knowledge and move up to a bigger scale. It was at her graduate school class that she met a man named Paul Christos. Paul was an honest man. Sheila did not wear her wedding ring in most public places. Paul never had any idea that Sheila was married. After several months of friendly communication, the two started an affair on a grand scale. Sheila would frequently find excuses to come home later than normal from school. Paul was falling madly in love with Sheila, as she was him. Sheila knew that she could not divorce Farid, as it would be a disgrace to her family. After several months of sneaking around, Farid found out of Sheila's affair. He immediately filed for divorce and flushed her out of his life.

In 2000, Paul and Sheila married and moved into an upscale condominium. The location of the condo was 21 Foxwood Drive, Pleasantville, New York. The location of their residence would prove to be vital to the case.

Sheila seemed to be settled down in her new life. She was married to a man of her choosing, at her time. She had obtained a great job as a research scientist at Purdue Pharma in Stamford, Connecticut. This job was something that she had always wanted. She had always valued education and, to her family, this was the culmination of those efforts. However, something else would catch her attention at this new job.

Also working at Purdue Pharma was a man named Nelson Sessler. Sessler was a highly intelligent man. He was a lead scientist for the company and someone that had established a strong reputation of hard work, dedication, and integrity. When Sheila met Nelson Sessler, the two immediately hit it off. They were always working together and hanging out together on their breaks throughout the day. It was apparent to anyone that the two were flirting and very personal together. In a similar situation, Nelson Sessler had no idea that she was married.

Sheila Davalloo went to great lengths to protect her marriage and work from her affair. The lies she maintained and the stories she made her husband to believe were nothing short of strange and demented. Sheila became extremely enamored with Nelson. The pair had struck up a steamy affair that really had no limits. Sheila was desperate to establish a secondary life with Nelson Sessler. To do this, she convinced her husband Paul Christos to leave their house while still staying "happily" married. Davalloo told him that her schizophrenic brother would be staying over at their house. She named this brother Shahiem. Shahiem had no idea that she was living with anyone and would lose his sanity if he knew. At least, that is what Sheila told Paul. Paul didn't necessarily understand the odd request, but was happy to oblige to help his wife. Paul Christos packed up all of his belongings and moved in with his parents. This was odd to everyone around the situation.

Upon Paul leaving to his parent's house, Sheila Davalloo hid anything and everything that would give any indication that she was married. Shahiem obviously didn't exist. Shahiem was in all actuality Nelson Sessler. Sheila invited Sessler to stay over. Nelson was honestly a bit suspicious of the whole situation. Sheila convinced Nelson that she was divorced and happily single. While Nelson did not live with Sheila at this point, he spent many nights at Davalloo's home and they continued a steamy, one-sided affair.

Sheila was an educated woman who had progressed rapidly in her career. She understood human thinking at a high level, and understood that she had problem. At the beginning of 2002, she began to see a psychiatrist. She was still respectful of her marriage to a point that she didn't want to divorce Paul, however she admitted in September of 2002 that she always maintained a fantasy with Nelson. Her affair continued. Her communications with her psychiatrist would prove to be crucial after her crimes and would be used to find the true facts to her mindset in the case.

On Sunday, March 23, 2003, Sheila and Paul were spending a quiet afternoon relaxing at their home. Their marriage had been slowly pressing on, however their love life had almost screeched to an immediate halt. Sheila suggested that they play a game that she had learned at work. Sheila was becoming very flirtatious, so Paul was fully up to agree to the game. The pretext of the game, she described, was that he had to be handcuffed and blindfolded. Thinking this was going to turn into a romantic, kinky sex game, he readily agreed. Little did he know what was about to happen. Sheila lavishly blindfolded Paul and handcuffed his hands behind his back. Sheila was about to do the unthinkable.

Sheila Davalloo produced a 4 inch long paring knife from the kitchen. She violently stabbed her husband, Paul Christos, in the chest. The stabbing fully penetrated his chest, sinking the blade over 3 ½ inches into his chest cavity. Immediately, Paul panicked and begged her to stop. Sheila screamed out that it had been an accident. She was ever convincing and Paul was super naïve. He begged her to let him out of the handcuffs, however Sheila claimed that she lost the key to the handcuffs. Paul Christos lay there bleeding out, his life hanging by a thread and contingent on receiving medical attention.

Paul began to tell Sheila to call 911. Sheila left the room to call 911, and returned minutes later and told Paul that the line was busy. Paul was still handcuffed at this time. He had been stabbed in the heart, and was literally bleeding to death internally. Next, Sheila tried to get a doctor that was nearby to come to the house. She left the house for over ten minutes, but returned only to find Paul still alive. She told him that the doctor was closed. She the magically found the handcuff keys. She released Paul from the handcuffs and took the blindfold off of him. In her mind, she thought that he would be dead soon.

Sheila Davalloo loaded Paul into the back of her car. He was clinging to life, and seemed to be fading rapidly. She calmly and slowly drove to the hospital. Ironically enough, she didn't even go to the emergency room when she arrived at the hospital. Paul was begging her to hurry up. In Paul's mind, this was still an accident. He still believed that Sheila didn't mean to stab him with the knife. He would quickly learn the truth in a matter of minutes.

Upon arriving at the hospital, Sheila bypassed the emergency room entrance and instead parked the car at a secluded lot far towards the back of the hospital. She exited the front door of the car, and opened the back door. At approximately 5:30 P.M. Sheila stabbed her husband Paul Christos a third time, severely piercing his heart. This would be a near lethal wound. This time, however, there was a witness to the event. An onlooker from the Behavioral Health Center saw the confrontation taking place between Davalloo and Christos. The onlooker immediately called 911 to get help to the scene. Davalloo fled the scene and left Christos for dead in the back of her car. Davalloo was found by the authorities and quickly rushed into the emergency room. He was put to the top of the line and urgently taken into the operating room where he would undergo extensive open heart surgery.

The onlooker seeing the confrontation ultimately saved Paul Christos's life. Without the call, Sheila likely would have left him for dead in the back of that car and he would have been dead in minutes. Sheila also saved his life herself by taking him to the hospital. Hopeful that this would clear her name and prove it to be some sort of accident, she believed that he would not make it to the hospital. When he was still clinging to life upon their arrival there, she decided to stab him again to finish the job. Ultimately, the fact that he was so close to the hospital is the only way he managed to survive this brutal stabbing. Had this wound happened at their home, he likely wouldn't have even made it to the hospital alive.

In a further twist of irony in this already wildly bizarre case, Sheila Davalloo actually fled the scene AND CAME BACK! She fled the scene after stabbing Paul for the third time in her car. She came back to get Paul out of the hospital. She screamed at hospital personnel demanding they release him to her. Police were notified and rushed to catch her before she could escape. Unfortunately, she escaped out of the hospital. Police finally caught up with her. She was arrested by Mount Pleasant police. They took her to the primary jurisdiction, which was the Westchester Police Department. She was finally in custody. Paul was given a 50 percent chance to live through the recovery of the surgery. His body was in an extremely fragile state and his heart had been badly injured. While the surgery had successfully stopped the bleeding and fixed the apparent injuries, the trauma had taken quite a toll. Paul was left in intensive care to recover from his devastating attack. Police questioning would yield a strong sense of confusion and anger as they struggled to get any sort of truth from Sheila.

Police of the Westchester Police Department began their questioning of Sheila Davalloo that evening. She was questioned most literally all night. Police statements describe Sheila as being unwilling to vacate her story of it all being an accident. She initially explained that Paul's injuries were not even inflicted by her. Her story stated that his injuries were caused when he was working in New York City. This was an outlandish story obviously, however police investigated quickly to determine there was no truth to this. Nonetheless, police had enough evidence to hold her in jail with no bail set. This was crucial for the rest of the investigation.

Investigators needed to talk with Paul Christos to get his testimony. However, while he was recovering and looked as though he would survive the horrific incident, he was obviously in no condition to give credible information. Police needed his story, however they were forced to wait. Investigators looked to other sources to acquire more evidence and, perhaps, an explanation to this unbelievable act.

The police investigation team decided it would be a good idea to look at her cell phone records. Sheila had told investigators that she tried to call 911. She was adamant about this fact, being as how her story was based around a work incident that she tried to solve by taking Paul to the hospital. What police found was shocking. Police found out that she not only never called 911, she called someone by the name of "Nelson". This call took place at exactly 4:59 P.M. This means that she called "Nelson" during the stabbing. This was critical evidence to police.

Sheila Davalloo was vigorously questioned about "Nelson" and why this person would be called during the suspected accident timeframe. This was the only call she had made the entire time. Police found it suspicious that she not only lied about calling 911, but also that she only made a single phone call the entire time. Typically, when your husband has a catastrophic event such as this, or a workplace "accident" as she had suggested, then you would call some family to at least let them know what was going on. In such a dire situation, you would not load up the victim in the back of your car and park a quarter mile away from the emergency room entrance. While Sheila did not provide detail as to what was going on at this time or any sort of explanation, she did provide a solid piece of information. She declared to police that the man's last name was Sessler. This call was, in fact, to her lover Nelson Sessler. Police now had enough evidence to charge Sheila Davalloo. The following morning, she was officially charged with attempted murder in the first degree. Police now turned their attention to Nelson Sessler.

The following morning, March 26, 2003, Nelson Sessler was brought in for questioning in the case. Initially, he was believed to be a suspect. Police felt like he may have been an accomplice or "the help" within this heinous crime. Upon only a few minutes of questioning, police has informed Nelson Sessler that Davalloo was married to the victim, Paul Christos. Nelson Sessler genuinely had no idea. In all of the time they had been lovers, he had his suspicions, but none of them had been proven true. Sheila Davalloo had concealed this secret to him this entire time. Investigators asked him about the phone call that Sheila had made to him on the night of the stabbing. As grim as it is, he informed investigators that Sheila had asked him over for dinner that night around 8:30 P.M. This was a chilling declaration of the coldness of this crime. This also spoke to her true intentions with Paul; she wanted and expected to kill him. Nelson Sessler was cleared of any wrongdoing in the case. He was of no involvement in the crime, and Sheila herself agreed that he had not been at the house for weeks. This was the last piece of crucial evidence that police hoped would lead to the ultimate conviction of Sheila Davalloo for attempted murder of Paul Christos.

The final argument that the investigative team needed to make was a motive. To investigators, the motive became quite clear when looking back at the family history of Sheila as well as her previous marriage. To the Davalloo family, divorce was disgraceful. Sheila could not possibly divorce Paul and keep her spot in the family. She decided that if Paul had died, it would then make it respectable that she move on with her life. While this is a motive that could never be fully proven, police felt it offered the best explanation for the random attempted murder of her husband.

On February 4, 2004, Sheila Davalloo stood trial for attempted murder in the first degree for the stabbing of Paul Christos. The small courthouse in White Plains, New York was packed with people. This trial had drawn heavy regional attention and national attention as well.

Paul Christos, now recovered from his near fatal experience, explained to the courtroom that he had never before seen Sheila act so violently. He went into great detail of how she showed no urgency to help him with what he initially thought was a sick accident. He explained that she left him to die, handcuffed and blindfolded, and showed no worry for the entire situation. Davalloo pleaded not guilty in what appeared to be an impossible situation for her. The opening statement of the prosecution is one that littered newspapers around New York and regionally around the United States. They portrayed Sheila as a deceitful, extremely manipulative woman who had the intelligence to violently get what she wanted. They explained that she didn't want to shame her family with another divorce, so killing rather than walking away was her solution to save the embarrassment. The overall goal of the killing would be to successfully and peacefully remain with Nelson Sessler. To wrap up their statement, the prosecution team played the interrogation where Sheila lied repeatedly as to how Paul got his stab wounds. The opening statement, for all intents and purposes, tilted the case in the prosecution's favor beyond a doubt.

After a relatively short trial, the jury was set to deliberate and decide the fate of Sheila Davalloo. On February 18, 2004, jury deliberations began. The next morning, they had reached their decision. Before he read the verdict, Judge Thomas Dickerson told Sheila a chilling statement:

"You tried to kill your husband. You waited for him to die, and have lied over and over again. You are ultimately a dangerous threat to society."

Davalloo was then read her conviction. She was found guilty on attempted murder in the first degree as well as assault with a deadly weapon in the first degree.

"She is a very dangerous woman who thought she would get away with what she did," Alison Carpenter, a lead investigator on the case said. "I found her to be deceptive from the beginning. She is very calculating."

Davalloo's parents chose not to attend the trial. They had been shamed and felt completely embarrassed of their daughter's actions. Sheila did, ironically, maintain a close relationship with her in-laws. She was seen sitting with them during the breaks of the trial in hallways and meeting rooms. Ironically still, when court officials handcuffed her, she told them to give her purse to her mother-in-law.

The relationship between Sheila and Paul after the trial was one that would be impossible to predict. While Paul ultimately filed for divorce from Sheila, he maintained that he didn't want her to serve an extreme amount of jail time. He felt that she suffered from a severe mental illness and wanted her to get help for that. Even after being stabbed to the brink of death by Sheila, Paul still supported her and wanted her to get help. This speaks volumes to the man that Paul Christos was, as well as the deep spell that Sheila was able to cast on those that were close to her.

The judge did not provide a bail amount for Sheila. She was ordered to stay at the Westchester County Jail until her sentencing. Paul and others pleaded for her to not get a severe punishment. The minimum sentence in the state of New York for these charges was 5 years. On April 6, 2004, the judge sentenced Sheila Davalloo to the maximum sentence of 25 years. She was given no possibility of parole for the duration of the sentence. This was devastating, but most within the investigation and follow-up of the crime felt that it was a fitting punishment to such a cold blooded attempt at murder.

If this story ended there, it would be considered tragic. However, it does not. She was also involved in a successfully completed murder. The details of this one are chilling and really show that the judge got the sentencing right.

Sheila Davalloo was convicted in 2012 for the murder of Anna Lisa Raymundo. The murder happened on November 8, 2002. This was just 4 months before her attempted murder of husband Paul Christos.

Davalloo was dating Nelson Sessler at the same time that Sessler was dating Anna Lisa Raymundo. All three of them worked at Purdue Pharma together. When Sessler became involved with Raymundo, he ended his relationship with Davalloo. This enraged Sheila and left her seeking a solution. On November 8, 2002, at precisely 12:29 P.M. police received an anonymous phone call from a woman at a pay phone. The location of the phone was at a nearby restaurant on Shippan Avenue. This anonymous caller said that her neighbor was being viciously attacked by a large, light skinned male. Police went on to the condo to find the front door unlocked. When police opened the door, they were shocked to find the body of Anna Lisa Raymundo, lifeless and covered in blood, lying in the middle of the living room. The house was a mess. It was apparent to responders that there was a violent struggle that went on. Evidence to this included shattered glass all about, debris from all over the house, and blood spatters that were seemingly endless. High and low, it had all the look of a violent and heinous murder scene.

Autopsy records showed that Anna had been stabbed nearly 20 times. She had been severely beaten and had suffered a massive head trauma that likely knocked her unconscious. She also, mysteriously to police, had long hair in her hand. While this points to the struggle that police had suspected, it did not go with the initial figure that the anonymous caller had described.

In May of 2003, just 2 months after she was held for her attempted murder of Paul Christos, police announced that they were investigating a woman that Anna had worked with at Purdue. Since this announcement, evidence substantially mounted against one common person: Sheila Davalloo.

On November 6, 2007 Stamford police obtained a warrant to arrest Sheila Davalloo. Sheila was serving her sentence in New York for her attempted murder conviction. Police arrived at Bedford Hills Correctional Facility for Women where she was serving her 25 year sentence. They extradited her back to Connecticut to stand trial for the murder of Anna Lisa Raymundo on December 29, 2008.

Evidence against Sheila in this case was extensive. Most notably, security video shows her leaving Purdue Pharma shortly before 11 A.M. on the morning of the murder. DNA from bloodstains acquired at the scene matched both Sheila and Anna. The blood was found all over the house, but specifically a strong sample was found on two separate faucets around the house that show her efforts to clean the scene. The initial call that police received that day matches the voice of Sheila Davalloo. This was a chilling surprise in the case.

The extradition process for Sheila was not overly complicated. She agreed to be extradited to face trial for the murder of Anna Lisa Raymundo. She was initially tried on January 14, 2009 where she pleaded not guilty to the murder of Anna. After lengthy deliberation and a very odd trial, Sheila was ultimately found guilty of murdering Anna Lisa Raymundo and was sentenced to 50 years in a Connecticut State Prison.

Sheila still had to finish her initial sentence of 25 years, and then her 50 year sentence would start. She is set to be in jail until 2079. She will undoubtedly die in prison.

Sheila Davalloo has a story that is unique in that she naively believed that people would believe anything she said. This was held true by the lovers that she had in her life. The men that she was with all, undoubtedly, hung on to everything she said. She was able to carry on an affair for over 2 years without the other person even knowing that she was married. She convinced her husband, after stabbing him two times in the chest, that it was an accident. As crazy as this sounds, it is all fully true. The punishment that Sheila is currently serving is not near enough. Sheila Davalloo has proven to be one of the most vicious and naïve women of the past 20 years.

HUSBAND KILLER SHEENA EASTBURN

91

JAIMI WEST

Sheena Eastburn seemed to have the cards stacked against her from the start. She and Tim Eastburn were married young, when she had only just turned fifteen. The couple wed in 1990, although Tim was older, at twenty-one years of age. Talking many years later to the Joplin Globe, Alica Blevins- Sheena's mother- talked about how she should have guided her daughter's life differently, and put her on a different path.

"She was only 15 then. She was just a kid... Sheena was wild. I will admit that," she said. "For her and Tim, life was one big party. "She got herself in situations that got her into a lot of trouble. There were a lot of things that happened to her as a child that she never told me.

I just wish I could have done more for her when I had the chance. Maybe things would have turned out differently."

They were divorced a short two years later, which is often the case for couples married at such a young age.

While the divorce was described by friends as amicable, the couple maintained a sexual relationship over the years. Both were heavy drinkers, and took drugs together. In fact, whenever Sheena needed a fix, friends said, she would visit her ex-husband and provide sexual favours in return for drugs. The couple were still so close that they discussed remarriage.

Speaking about their relationship, Sheena would later say: "There were days when he loved me more than you could ever imagine and there were other days when we just fought. I was 15 years old when we got married. He was like a father and a husband to me. He was a wonderful man."

On or around November 1st, 1991, Sheena met Terry Banks for the first time, and the two immediately became close. When Banks learned of Sheena's continuing relationship with her ex-husband, however, he became "extremely possessive, jealous, and violent" according to court records. This was the catalyst for Tim's murder.

Tim Eastburn's murder

Tim was murdered using his own rifle, on November 19th 1992. He was shot in his own home in McDonald County, Missouri. The house is set a little back from the road, among the wooded hills common in McDonald County.

At the time of the murder, Sheena had only just turned seventeen, and her co-defendants were nineteen (Banks) and eighteen as well (Myers).

Two days previously, Sheena's co-defendants, Terry Banks and Matt Myers, had stolen Tim's gun- an AK-47- in a break-in along with a third man named Denashay, or 'D.J'. Johnson. They also took the chance to steal some of Tim's valuables, since stealing the gun on its own would have appeared suspicious.

The burglary took place only two weeks after Sheena had begun secretly dating her fellow co-defendant, Terry Banks. Tim and Sheena, Banks, Myers and Johnson were in fact all part of the same large circle of friends. In the time building up to the murder, the group had been drinking to excess and using drugs, a fact which probably gave the defendants the courage to do what they were about to do.

On the evening of November 19th, Sheena, Banks and Myers paid a visit to Tim at his home. It was only on that day that Sheena learned of the burglary at all; Myers and Banks had said they wanted to sell the gun- which would have fetched a good price- but Sheena convinced them not to, since it could be traced back to Tim through the serial number.

Sheena went in at first, alone, to talk with him. She asked him if he would like to come outside to take a ride on her motorbike, but he refused, saying that it was too late at night for him to want to go out.

At the time, Banks and Myers were hiding on the front porch. As Tim and Sheena continued talking, they walked through the house to the kitchen, where the pair kissed. It was only seconds later that Tim was shot with his own gun, through the window, by one of the pair outside. He quickly fell to the floor, and as he lay, Myers ran into the house to shoot him again to 'finish him off'. As he shot Tim for the second and final time, Sheena and Terry Banks ran from the house.

According to later interviews with Sheena, Tim's last words were "God forgive me for all my sins."

All three were arrested only days later, and each confessed separately to their role in Tim's murder. Each of their confessions were coherent, and none of the defendants contradicted the others with regards to their description of the day's events. However, Banks and Myers both claimed that Sheena had come up with the plot to murder Tim, a claim that she denied.

The Trial

Sheena was in prison for three years by the time she was finally put up for trial.

The facts of Tim Eastburn's murder were not challenged in court by either Terry Banks or Matt Myers. The only challenge made by Sheena was whether her actions were made after 'deliberation and cool reflection' or not- which is the metric by which murder in the first degree is judged under Missouri law. However, the defence also argued that Sheena did not necessarily understand her co-defendants' murderous intentions beforehand, a fact which also would have lessened the charge against her.

In testimony for her defence, Sheena claimed that she only learned of the burglary on the day of the murder itself. She believed that on the day that Tim died, the group of three were going to steal money and drugs from her ex-husband. She denied any knowledge of a plot to kill him. "I was supposed to go down there and get him out of the house, then we were going rob him for drugs and money."

They also planned to leave the gun at Tim's house after the robbery, rather than arouse suspicion by selling it. Sheena was quoted in interviews long after the trial, still standing by what she said. "The intent was to take back the gun that was stolen. They could track it down.

The timeline of the day's events suggested otherwise, however. Sheena's request for her ex-husband to follow her outside, and her bringing him to the kitchen with a window to the front of the house, suggested that she was trying to lead him to her death. At the very least, it was clear that it wasn't Sheena who fired the fatal shots from Tim's own gun. She claimed that Banks had shot him first in a fit of passion, after seeing the pair kiss. Myers had then delivered the final bullet.

After the shot was fired, Sheena said, "[w]e both dropped and when we dropped I crawled around to where he was, and I tried to stop the bleeding. There was nothing I could do." She was trying to paint a picture of innocence. She later talked about how she had tried to stop the bleeding with a towel and a sock that were lying nearby.

Over the course of the trial, extensive physical evidence was used in attempt to prove the group's guilt, almost sixty items in total. These included the rifle and the fragments of bullets found in Tim's body- which matched- and photo after photo of the crime scene.

D.J. Johnson also testified to the effect that the murder had been pre-meditated. He was actually a witness for the prosecution throughout the trial, as part of a plea bargain to help secure the verdicts of murder against the other three. As a result of his actions, he was given probation in connection to the charges of burglary against him, as he was part of the group that stole Tim's AK-47.

He testified that on the day of the murder itself, he overheard a three-way conversation between Myers, Banks and Sheena. In that conversation, Sheena discussed Tim with the others, claiming that he had raped her, and that she would love to see him dead. Banks, her then boyfriend, and Myers then both volunteered their services, according to Johnson. Sheena's attorneys made no attempt to discredit him, or disagree with any of his testimony.

The defence, however, argued that his testimony was unreliable due to its acquisition through a plea bargain. Johnson was offered freedom in exchange for his witness statements, and this perhaps did cast doubt on the truth of what he said. However, it was left for the jury to decide just what to make of his claims, and his statements formed a key part of the prosecution's case.

Prison Time

Whether the jury's decision would have been changed by any of this information must forever remain unknown. What they did decide, after a gruelling six hours, was that Sheena was guilty of first-degree murder.

Matt Myers was sentenced as the man who, according to the three confessions, had fired both of the fatal shots. Although he was only charged with second degree murder, among other offences related to Tim's murder (i.e. the burglary), he was sent to prison for a total of 67 years. Because of the murder being judged as of the second degree, he was eligible for parole throughout his sentence.

Terry Banks on the other hand, was sent to prison for life, on a charge of first degree murder. Sheena, too, was jailed with the same charge. The fact that Banks and Sheena were charged with first degree murder, whereas Myers (who fired one of the shots that killed Tim) wasn't, seems strange in hindsight. But Myers had made a plea bargain that saw him receive 'only' 67 years, but with the chance for parole in the future.

Indeed, Sheena's attorney filed a motion for post conviction relief in the immediate aftermath of the sentence, but this motion was denied.

"I really believed I was going to get second degree murder and I was accountable for that. I was okay with that," Sheena said in an interview, years later. She was visibly stunned when she learned of her sentence. "All I could hear was my mother in the courtroom... She was wailing," Sheena told KOAM TV. As part of the same news segment, Sheena's mother Alica Bleavins remembered the same scene: "I couldn't control it. When that's your child, and your only child, and your hands are tied..."

Terry Banks' story became more interesting in the year 2000, when he escaped from his maximum-security prison with the help of a guard. Lynnette Barnett smuggled Banks out in broad daylight, with the help of an old uniform and a fake ID. They were on the run for six weeks before they were caught. She was jailed for five years, with the help of video evidence and correspondence between her and Banks. She was, however, paroled within a year of her sentence.

Banks had another 16 years added to his sentence, although since he was already in prison for life with no option of parole, it makes little difference.

At the time of the escape, Sheena's mother said: "They put her on lock-down. They put her in the hole. They were going to leave her there until he was captured. The FBI, well, they were all over Sheena. She was the one who told them his dad was in Texas."

Signs of hope for Sheena?

There were several facts and allegations which weren't raised at trial, that in hindsight, should have been. Sheena's attorneys spoke publicly about how the outcome may have been completely different had they brought them up.

For one, IQ tests performed by Sheena in the buildup to the trial suggested that she would be incapable of organising the events as described by the prosecution.

There were also allegations that she had been raped by a McDonald County Jail when awaiting trial, and even taken to an abortion clinic. A guard who had been working there, Terrie Zornes, had been accused by Sheena of manipulating and raping her several times over the course of her time there. He had been 31, whereas she was still a minor.

Sheena claimed that he had taken her twice to the property room in 1994, and attacked her there. He was the only guard on duty at the time. According to interviews, Sheena had told her mother: "I told my mother that the officer had taken me to a property closet and had sex with me. She flipped out at that point. They locked me down in my cell. Cut off my phone. I wasn't allowed to talk to anybody. They cut off my visitors."

Multiple reviews of the surveillance tape from the nights that Sheena alleged she had been raped gave suspicious results. While nothing of note happened, at one point in the recordings the clock would jump forward. "The hands on the clock jumped forward. A clock doesn't do that," The Sheriff of McDonald County Jail later said.

The Sherriff had nonetheless defended Zornes, claiming that the sex was "consensual". Altogether, it seemed as if both the guard and the Sheriff felt that there was something to hide.

Sheena responded with revealing comments about her past. "They kept trying to tell me it was consensual. They said: 'You know you wanted it. You know you miss it.' It was not like I fought it because there was no way I could have stopped him. I have experienced sexual abuse all of my life. I have been raped before in a violent way. After you have been in that situation, you just learn it's easier to let it go and not fight."

Moreover, in the years since the case was closed, Myers recanted on his testimony at the trial that Sheena had been the mastermind of the operation. Kent Gipson, Sheena's long time attorney, had even attained an affidavit to that effect- and that he had acquired the same from Johnson, too. This would mean that in conjunction with their defence stemming from the low IQ test score, it would be possible to argue that Sheena could not have possibly wanted Tim to be killed that day.

These facts all gave Sheena hope that she could appeal her sentence, and perhaps, win. Even if she were only able to replace her sentence with one for second degree murder, she would at least be eligible for parole in the end.

Supreme Court challenge

In interviews after her sentencing, Sheena said: "I still thought that I might get out of prison someday... I didn't realize that life without parole actually meant life without parole." She continued to maintain her innocence, saying that she had never planned a murder that day, only a robbery.

In 2012, a case went through the Alabama Supreme Court which found that the sentence of life without parole was actually unconstitutional when handed down to a minor. The case came from Alabama, but because it had been decided by the Supreme Court, cases could now be challenged nationwide. Missouri, at the time, had 84 cases of juveniles jailed for life without parole and each one of them could now seek to have their sentences reduced.

Suddenly, it seemed that Sheena might have found a way out. Once more, Sheena contacted her attorney, and they began to prepare her case for appeal. Talking to KOAM TV, her attorney Kent Gipson said "I think if you look across the spectrum of persons convicted of first degree murder, I'd say her level of culpability is among the lowest I've ever seen."

Sheena's attorney believed that she had a great chance to finally be considered for parole; and both clearly believed that she deserved the chance. "I think inevitably she will be given a parolable sentence and will be given a chance to get out of prison," Gipson said at the time. Speaking about the progress she had made while in prison, he said "She's obviously not the same person she was when she was 17 years old, I don't think any of us are... She is probably the most ideal candidate for parole any of them [prison staff] have ever seen.""

Miles Parks, a retired investigator who had worked on the case, disagreed. "Sheena Eastburn was old enough to get a driver's license, old enough to get married, old enough to know the difference between right and wrong," Parks said. "What do you think is the appropriate punishment?"

In an interview before her appeal with KOAM TV, she talked about the possibility that she might be released. "I came to that realization a long time ago, and I gave it to God, and I got peace," she had said. She still maintained that she had no role in Tim's murder, saying that "[t]here was no reason for Tim to die... None."

With her interviewer, she discussed what she missed about the outside world: "...going down to the refrigerator in the middle of the night and being able to get what you want. Walking barefoot on grass somewhere that it doesn't say 'out of bounds'. Going outside after dark. Just taking time to experience free, fresh air... I know it smells different on the other side."

Sheena wished that she could somehow find release. But she still refused to get her hopes up, stating that "You never count on anything completely until it happens because you can't let yourself get your hopes too high and then be devastated all the time. It's just a hard way to live." Over her time in prison, she had clearly lived with a hope that one day she would be set free, but had only been disappointed.

The Post-Conviction Hearing

Close friends and relatives of Tim's did not want the case re-opened. Speaking in an interview, Bobby Eastburn said, "We have been keeping track of it. We don't like what is going on. She worked hard to get in there and we don't want her out of prison. "My brother won't get a second chance. She's apparently trying to get a second chance. They say she was suffering from PTSD because of her childhood and that she was not very smart. She manipulated the situation to kill Tim. She was the mastermind behind it. She was intelligent enough to set the whole situation up."

On April 30th of 2013, three cases of minors jailed for life were put before the Missouri Supreme Court- one of them being Sheena's. Her attorney argued that the original motion that had been filed way back in 1992, for post conviction relief, should not have been denied. They argued that the judge should have then realised that such a sentence was unconstitutional.

The state argued that they did not then have the authority to challenge the constitutionality of the sentence, and so they were correct to not have allowed the defendant's motion for relief. After both sides had been presented, the court took recess so that the judges could decide on their fate.

"I am definitely guilty of second-degree murder," Sheena said in an interview around the time of her appeal.

But whether or not her appeals would be successful, she felt all along that she could never be free. "For somebody with a case like this, the prison is not really the prison. It's always going to be inside. You will always be in prison. It does not matter whether you are free or locked up, I think you will always have that inside."

But on Tuesday 25th July, that year, the Missouri Supreme Court returned the unanimous verdict that her appeal did not stand. Based on the facts of the case, they still argued that it was necessary for Sheena to be imprisoned for life.

Sheena's final hearing

It turned out that Sheena would eventually win her appeal after all.

In 2015, Sheena appealed again, under the same Supreme Court ruling as before. In her hearing of October that year, she sought the sentence of second degree murder through a plea agreement with the prosecutor. To do so, Eastburn had to waive any and all post-conviction and appeal rights- which she did.

The hearing was only 25 minutes long in total this time around. Lou Kelling, a former sheriff and supporter of Eastburn's release on parole, said at the appeal, "This is what she should have been charged with to begin with. She was an accessory to the crime. She served 10 years more time than she should have served. That on top of the fact that she was mistreated while in custody."

The defence had indeed used the same arguments as in the prior appeal, including the evidence of Sheena's IQ test, and allegations of rape and forced abortion. This time, the court decided to vacate the prior judgement. Since she had been in prison for more than 23 years, the agreement made her immediately eligible for a parole hearing.

Parole at last

Sheena Eastburn is now set to be released from prison in November, 2017. She has been judged to have served her time for second degree murder, and is getting ready for life on the outside for the first time in her life as an adult.

In a telephone interview with the Joplin Globe after it became common knowledge that she was set to be released, Eastburn said: "I now know when I will be able to move on with my life. I am grateful for a chance at parole."

In the same interview, she described how she was planning to write to the parole board and the governor in the hope that she could demonstrate just how much she had changed during her time locked away from society. "I want to show that I can be successful outside of the prison," she said. "I am very sorry for the things that happened. I have changed my life and will make better choices."

In another interview, she described her plans for the outside world. "I would go to school to become a certified personal trainer. I would love to minister to juveniles and help them know that the choices we do make have a consequence. I really do want to help people. I know that sounds crazy. But I want to help and let them know there are other choices out there no matter what your life is like because I had a bad life and childhood, but I still had choices. I did not realize that then."

And it did indeed seem that she had made genuine effort to turn her life around. In a separate interview, Sheena's mother claimed that her daughter had made every effort she possibly could from within the prison system. "Sheena has completed all of the classes that they offer at the prison. She has taken everything ... She'll sit there and the taxpayers will pay $80,000 a year to feed and house her. If she had been let out, she'd have a job and feed herself. This is something I don't understand. But we are still grateful to have a release date."

"We have waited a long time for this day to come, but we don't know when she will be released. We don't have an out day yet," Blevins said. "It could be just a matter of some paperwork. No one can really say right now."

During her time in prison, Sheena had begun full time work as an obedience trainer for rescue dogs. On top of this full time job, she had also become a qualified aerobics instructor, and found occasional work in prison helping disabled inmates. On occasion, she even led victim counselling sessions. She had spent her time as wisely as she could, and it had given her inspiration for her future release.

Before her first appeal on the unconstitutional nature of her sentence, her attorney had said "Maturity and education, things like that, should be taken into account and that's all we're really asking, that she be given the opportunity to prove to the parole board and other people that she deserves a second chance."

By the end of this year, she will be getting that chance.

HUSBAND KILLER DONNA YAKLICH

104

JESSI DIXON

Old-fashioned police work

In December 1985, a narcotics detective was shot and killed in the driveway of his farm in Pueblo, Colorado, where he lived with his five children and his wife, Donna Yaklich. Initially, authorities suspected Dennis' death was linked to his work in law enforcement, but a tip led them to two teenage shooters – and eventually, back to Dennis' wife, Donna.

However, attorneys for Donna Yaklich argued that Dennis had been beating his wife. The murder, they claimed, was a battered woman's desperate attempt to escape a lifetime of abuse – or potentially becoming a murder victim herself, like Dennis' first wife, who is thought to have died of a diet drug overdose in 1977.

Yaklich was finally acquitted of first-degree murder after a mistrial and a second trial that has been described as "grueling," but was convicted on the charge of conspiracy for hiring gunmen to kill her husband. Her sentence was forty years in prison, but was released to a halfway house in 2005, after serving close to eighteen years.

The young men Yaklich had hired to carry out the murder were also arrested and sentenced. Charles Greenwell, who was only 16 when the crime was committed, received a sentence of twenty years while his brother Eddie, who had been 25, received thirty years.

However, while Yaklich's claims of abuse weren't enough to get her off on the premise of self-defence, they did encourage authorities to reopen their investigation into the death of Barbara Yaklich. According to a cold case team, the investigation was "incomplete."

"This case needed some good, old-fashioned police work," said team lead Steve Johnson, with the Colorado Bureau of Investigation. "In my opinion, I have seen better documented traffic accidents."

Discrepancies were found in the autopsy report, which originally claimed Barbara had fainted from taking diet pills. When her body-builder husband, Dennis, tried "energetically" to resuscitate her, she suffered bleeding in her abdomen. However, administering CPR is not an appropriate reaction to fainting – and as a police officer trained in CPR, Dennis would have known this.

Still, there was apparently no examination of the potential crime scene, and when Dennis was asked to take a polygraph to support his defense, he refused.

Denver-area pathologist Michael Doberson determined that the conclusions in the report were "very unusual" – the internal damage Barbara had suffered, he claimed, was more likely caused by a blow to the abdomen. Doberson included his findings in a letter to Johnson dated in 2005, stating that in his opinion, "the entire scenario is simply not credible." A second forensic pathologist concurred with Doberson's conclusions.

According to reports, Barbara's liver tore open and her abdomen was quickly filled with more than 2,000 millilitres of blood – nearly 40 per cent of her total blood volume, and more than twice as much as is typical in a victim of a fatal car accident.

Investigators are now considering her death as "suspicious," with the tear caused by a blunt force trauma consistent with "punches and knee drops to the upper abdomen," according to pathologist Stephen Cina. However, the autopsy report showed no other indications that would reveal a pattern of abuse – no recorded discoloration, bruising, or external signs of beatings.

While the investigation into Barbara's death is now complete, the case hasn't been closed. According to the coroner and the Pueblo County Sheriff, the public deserves answers to the questions that have been raised.

The family man

Donna Yaklich met Dennis and his children only a few months after Barbara's death. According to Yaklich, the plan was to move in with the family for the summer and help him get the kids back into their home, since they were temporarily staying with Dennis' mother.

"I had no expected to fall in love with the children, who so desperately needed someone," Yaklich said. "They were grieving for their mother, so I couldn't bear to leave them."

Barbara had died on Valentine's Day, and had "appeared fine" as her children left for school that morning. However, an hour later, Barbara was dead – and Dennis was the only person who had been with her as she died. According to some reports, there are members of the community who do continue to question Dennis' involvement in the death of his first wife, including at least one of his former co-workers.

"Dennis' fellow officers knew he was out of control, but they also knew when they needed him he would be the first to go through the door," Yaklich said. "No one who worked with him would go against him."

It was this feeling of hopelessness that eventually led Yaklich to hire gunmen to kill her husband, in an effort to finally end the ongoing abuse. She'd moved in with Dennis when she was only 22 and he was 30. The children were aged 3, 9, 11, and 12 – and she immediately fell into the role of step-mother, despite the abuse which began only a month after Yaklich moved in. She said she attempted to leave a few times, but always went back.

"I feared Dennis, but at the same time I felt at home with him because I had grown up in an abusive environment," Yaklich said. "I fell into the trap of thinking if I could make everything perfect for him, he wouldn't get mad at me or at the kids. Dennis' threats to kill me or kill someone I loved if I ever left again kept me there."

Dennis even threatened to use his access to federal law enforcement agents against Yaklich, telling her that she'd never be able to get away from him – these agents were capable of fiding anyone, anywhere. Eventually, she said, "I lost myself. I lost hope."

"I became very depressed and mad at myself because I had no trusted my instincts about leaving the relationship when the abuse started," Yaklich said. "Suicidal thoughts became an answer. Then came homicidal thoughts."

Looking back, Yaklich admitted that she wished she had listened to those first instincts, but eventually came to a point where she no longer cared. However, she said she has been working on bettering herself since being convicted and sentenced.

"Being in prison is similar to the prison I put myself in while I was married to Dennis," she said. "However, prison is also what you make of it, so I've enrolled in educational programs, had therapy, and also taken care of myself. Things I should have done in society."

A professional abuser

At a menacing 6'5" and 280 pounds, Dennis Yaklich was a competitive weightlifter who continuously used steroids to supplement his workouts – despite the fact that they also enhanced his aggressive tendencies. While the officers who worked with him conceded that he was always the go-to guy for breaking down a door or clearing a room, he was difficult to manage. In fact, when he did become confrontational, even a supervisor threatened to shoot him because they had no other way to defend themselves.

A former partner once stated that he felt he always had to "clean up after Dennis," and other co-workers have admitted they "dreaded" working with Dennis, because of his aggressive and unpredictable behaviour. Some of his closest colleagues have even confessed that Dennis displayed some "abusive tactics" on the job – while denying the complaints of citizens against him.

Yaklich endured what can only be described as domestic terrorism. While the physical abuse, which included slapping, choking, kicking, and pushing her down stairs as well as sadistic sexual assaults, was indeed disabling and troubling, the psychological abuse was almost worse. According to Yaklich, the threat of death loomed constantly – Dennis would put his gun to her head and threaten to kill her, point his finger at her in the shape of a gun and blow on it after miming shooting her with it, and even beating her under the cover of darkness so she wouldn't be able to prepare for the blows.

The physical abuse has been corroborated by a number of independent witnesses, including a mailman who reported seeing bruises on Yaklich's face, and a telephone repairman who had been called in twice to fix phones after Dennis had yanked them out of the wall in a fit of rage.

Following Yaklich's arrest, the repairman spoke with detectives investigating Dennis' death and said the bruises he had seen on Yaklich's neck and cheek were so prominent, he noticed them "at a glance." The detective inquired how the repairman could recall the incident so vividly, and he admitted that in his line of work, he sees "a lot of things like that in the low income areas and the projects, but I was shocked to see a cop's wife all bruised up like she was."

Cries unheard

Yaklich's first documented attempt for police intervention came in 1982, when she called Dennis' partner to explain that Dennis was "out of control" and threatening to kill her. The detective advised her to leave right away, but she said she was too afraid – if she left, she said, Dennis had told her he would kill her entire family, starting with her father.

Believing that Yaklich was in fear for her life, the detective immediately went to inform his supervisor about the call he'd received about his partner. According to the detective, the supervisor had gestured to indicate that he should just forget the call – it was none of their business – and the incident went unreported.

It was then that Yaklich realized that trying to get help from the police would be completely futile, and she would need to seek support elsewhere.

The next year, in November of 1983, Yaklich endured a short and traumatic visit with a psychologist. After Yaklich "sobbed uncontrollably" through the entire session, the psychologist recommended she leave her husband – but failed to offer her suggestions to muster the courage needed to do so, or what steps she could take to do it safely.

Since Yaklich was required to provide her abusive husband with detailed accounts of where she spent all her time, there was no way for her to continue therapy with regular appointments. She never went back for another session.

A few months later, Yaklich escaped to a battered women's shelter in Denver, in February of 1984. Dennis pleaded with her to come home, and even went so far as to promise that he would try to change – and because she was ashamed to go back to him again, Yaklich told the counselors that she was leaving the state.

Still, the abuse hadn't stopped another year later. Early in 1985, Yaklich tried talking to friends and family members – telling them she needed advice because Dennis was going to kill her. These claims were shrugged off by everyone she turned to, and the abuse began to escalate.

Feeling as though she had no other options, Yaklich began looking for an opportunity to kill herself. Her attempts failed, however, when she realized she would be abandoning her young son and step-children with their abusive father – and after witnessing the struggles of Barbara's children as they grieved the loss of their mother, she was unable to force that situation on her own child.

Later that year, the Pueblo Sheriff's Department received a 911 call from Yaklich's mother. One of the step-children had called Yaklich's parents after hearing what they thought was Dennis pushing Yaklich through a plate glass window. While it turned out that the noise was caused by just a bowl hitting the floor, the officers who responded barely acknowledged Yaklich.

In fact, their inspection of the situation involved a brief conversation with Dennis followed by a tour of the gym Dennis was building on the property. The situation only reinforced Yaklich's desperate situation on the other side of the blue line – living in fear of an abusive spouse with no support or protection from the authorities.

Finally, on December 12, 1985, one of Yaklich's friends finally responded to her pleas for help. A neighbour, Eddie Greenwell, waited at the Yaklich family's farm with his younger brother, Charles, into the early morning hours. When Dennis returned home after working a night shift, the brothers shot and killed him. Yaklich was inside the house, sleeping.

According to court documents, Yaklich had "approached several people" in an attempt to have her husband killed, and had met with Eddie Greenwell many times over a period of eight months. The Greenwell brothers were paid $4,200 in installments after the murder was committed – although the brothers testified they had been promised $45,000.

The story of the tragic marriage was detailed in a made-for-television movie called *Cries Unheard: The Donna Yaklich Story*. The film was released in 1994 and starred former Charlie's Angel Jaclyn Smith as Yaklich.

A disturbing conflict of interest

After Dennis was killed, the Pueblo Police Department – Dennis' employer – carried out an investigation into his death, despite the fact that the murder actually took place in the jurisdiction of the Pueblo Sheriff's Office. Lead roles in the inquiry were awarded to narcotics detectives – Dennis' partners.

The District Attorney was also a personal friend of Dennis', and even admitted to being a material witness in his own case. At the time of the trial, DA Sandstrom was wrapped up in a highly contested election – and this clear political agenda, combined with the attempts of the police department to hide its role in Yaklich's abuse and ultimately, Dennis' death, indicate incredible prejudice against Yaklich from the very beginning.

Not that Yaklich was surprised. After attempting to secure the help of police several times during the course of her abusive marriage, it was obvious to Yaklich that law enforcement was not on her side.

Still, the jury acquitted Yaklich of the charge of first-degree murder. Several jurors even thought Yaklich deserved to be acquitted of all charges, but felt intimidated by the Pueblo Police Department – and feared potential retaliation. Instead, the jury voted guilty on the charge of conspiracy to commit murder, believing that the fair-minded judge would give the battered wife the minimum sentence of eight years.

The probation supervisor who had conducted Yaklich's pre-sentencing investigation testified that Yaklich would be an "excellent candidate" for sentencing alternatives outside of the Department of Corrections, and gave the court his recommendation for the minimum sentence. His testimony affirmed the sense of desperation Yaklich claimed to be struggling with.

"I really felt that whether they did what she wanted done, to have Dennis killed, or whether Dennis found out and killed her, it didn't matter," he said. "She was at a point in her life where either was satisfactory."

However, the late Judge Seavy who presided over the trial chose to overlook the circumstances leading to Dennis' murder and remanded Yaklich to the Department of Corrections for a sentence of forty years. According to the judge, Yaklich "started this whole scenario," and therefore deserved to serve a period of time "in excess of the longest Greenwell's sentence."

"We cannot overlook the fact that Yaklich's participation in the death of her husband was not merely peripheral," stated court documents. "Had it not been for Yaklich, the Greenwells would not have been involved in this murder. Thus, in our view, we would be establishing poor public policy if Yaklich were to escape punishment by virtue of an unprecedented application of self-defense while the Greenwells were convicted of murder."

Still, the jurors were shocked and horrified by the severity of Judge Seavy's harsh sentence. More than half of the serving jurors submitted letters expressing their disappointment with the resulting sentence to a judge who presided over Yaklich's sentencing reconsideration a few years later. These letters were dismissed by that judge, however, who felt "that they must not allow for personal sympathy to influence their decision." Several of the jurors who served on the initial trial event went on to diligently advocate for Yaklich's early release, eighteen years later.

According to Dr. Lenore Walker, who counseled and evaluated Yaklich and provided expert testimony at her trial, Judge Seavy was "using the court and a woman's life to express his own ignorance of a battered woman's plight."

The conspiracy

According to court documents, Yaklich did receive payments totalling more than $250,000 under her late husband's three life insurance policies – leading to a theory that the motivation that pushed her to arrange her husband's death was to obtain this insurance money. The defense argued that Yaklich suffered from "battered woman syndrome," and that the conspiracy to commit murder was a "justifiable act of self-defence ... committed under duress resulting from years of physical and psychological battering by her husband."

"Yaklich lived in a constant state of fear of her husband," the defense argued. "At the time of his death, she believed she was in imminent danger of being killed by him or receiving great bodily injury from him."

The defense went on to explain that many battered women are unable to safely leave their abusive spouses – and in fact, the abuse often escalates as a result of a separation. Abusers have also been known to pursue their victims after they've left, subjecting them to "brutal attacks."

"Additionally, battered women may not psychologically or emotionally have the alternative of leaving the abuser because of their low self-esteem, their emotional and economic dependency, the absence of another place to go, and the woman's legitimate fear of the abuser's response to her leaving," stated the defense. "Battered women become trapped in their own fear and often feel that their only recourse is to kill the batterer or be killed."

Several people involved with the case, including District Attorney Sandstrom, have stated that if Yaklich had gone ahead and committed the murder herself, "she would have walked." However, the DA and many others also question the validity of Yaklich's testimony, including that Dennis was abusing her – maintaining the theory that Yaklich conspired to have him killed just to receive the insurance money.

The DA even stated that "if she had shot him herself, there would be no issue" – leading some to wonder if Sandstrom sees money as an acceptable motive for murder, as long as you follow through with it on your own.

Like most battered women, Yaklich both loved and hated her husband. Killing him herself would have been difficult, as she was afraid that as soon as she pointed a gun at him to save herself and her children, the love she had for him would "override her fear of him," and cause her to second-guess her decision. The ramifications from that could have bene deadly.

Another concern for Yaklich was her husband's established persona of invincibility – one he had carefully instilled in her over years of repeated psychological and physical abuse. Not only did Yaklich struggle to trust in her own ability to kill her husband, she struggled to believe that he would ever really die.

One of the prosecution's expert witnesses, Dr. Alice Brill, said in her testimony that Yaklich didn't meet the traditional profile of a battered woman. These women, according to Brill, generally kill their spouses with little premeditation and show little interest in pursuing relationships with other men – while Yaklich spent at least ten months planning her husband's murder, and had had at least one extramarital affair about a year before Dennis was killed.

Dennis' children also continue to question Yaklich's testimony, stating that none of them had ever witnessed any physical abuse from Dennis during the eight years of the couple's marriage. After Yaklich's parole hearing in October 2005, Dennis' daughter Vanessa fought back tears while talking about the court's decision to release Yaklich after she'd only served eighteen years of her forty-year sentence.

"It's devastating – I don't believe justice has prevailed," she said. "My father died at age 38. He was stripped of his opportunity to live life. He was prevented from raising his children, from seeing us grow up and accomplishing our goals."

Vanessa stated that Yaklich's claims of beatings and abuse were "an outright lie" – and that the depiction of the family's life shown in the TV-movie *Cries Unheard* were based entirely on prison interviews with Yaklich herself, with no supporting evidence or facts contributed by other relatives or friends.

Vanessa added that just two months before her father was killed, Yaklich had told her that Dennis had asked for a divorce – but that the couple planned to delay the proceedings until after the Christmas holidays, for the sake of the younger children. This story has been corroborated by Dennis' brother, who said Dennis told him over the phone that he planned to divorce Yaklich once the holidays had passed.

"(Dennis') life was taken because he was going to divorce my step-mother and not because she was the victim of abuse," Vanessa said. "I never feared my father, nor did I observe any abuse, whether it be psychological or physical, perpetrated by him. His demeanor was calm and loving, his words encouraging and supportive. I can honestly state my step-mother did not provide my siblings or myself with the same."

According to Vanessa, Yaklich didn't show any grief or remorse after Dennis had been killed – and even slapped Vanessa when she began to cry at her father's funeral. She went on to detail the ongoing "injustice," claiming to defend her father since he is no longer able to defend himself.

"My stepmother's legal defense was paid for by my father's life insurance proceeds and my family and I believe she profited from the made-for-television monstrosity," Vanessa said. "Most recently, her financial status has provided her with the ability to hire a media publicist."

Questions also remain about the relationship Yaklich had with her defense attorney, John Giduck. Records show Giduck and Yaklich took a romantic vacation to Jamaica together prior to her arrest in March 1986 – a getaway funded entirely from the death benefit Yaklich received after having her husband murdered.

In fact, the vacation was cut short when Yaklich was notified of the charges that were being brought against her, and surrendered to police upon her return to Pueblo. Most of the insurance money had already been spent by the time Yaklich was arrested.

According to information reported in the Colorado Springs Gazette, Yaklich had been involved in an extramarital affair about a year before Dennis' murder, and had begun a romantic relationship with Giduck only weeks after her husband's death. Giduck had apparently attended Dennis' funeral, where he had given Yaklich his business card and told him to call if she needed anything.

Yaklich reached out to him a few days later, after police asked her to verify the statement she'd given with a routine polygraph test.

A safe and abuse-free life

Still, Yaklich had a spotless record prior to her incarceration, which continued even after she was sent to prison – a testament to her strength of character. According to prison records, Yaklich managed to vigilantly avoid conflict and strictly followed the many rules surrounding prison life. Despite being forced into an environment filled with trouble, Yaklich managed to stay out of it through her entire eighteen-year term.

During her incarceration, Yaklich obtained an associate's degree as well as a Bachelor's degree in psychology – while working in maintenance and then in a computer-refurbishing program at the correctional facility. According to staff there, Yaklich was a hard and industrious worker, even volunteering her time as a member of the Fire Response Team, comprised of prisoners trained in firefighting and first aid.

Yaklich has also volunteered with several programs that support victims of abuse, earning high praise from her Department of Corrections supervisors regarding the effectiveness of her work with young people. She encourages victims of domestic abuse to seek support from therapy groups to find the strength to break away from an abusive partner – to learn how to stay away emotionally and physically.

"Educating ourselves about the issues and statistics relative to domestic violence will help us pass this information on to the next generation," Yaklich said. "Our children need to learn that they have the right to safe and abuse-free lives."

HUSBAND KILLER MICHELLE REYNOLDS

GARY GUIDEN

On July 5th, 2004, a Frito Lay delivery pulled into the empty parking lot of a distribution center in Rome, Georgia. The man noticed that another man- one he didn't recognize- was coming out of the office, and although someone in the office in the early morning hours wasn't unusual, not recognizing the man was. According to the diver, the man who came into view appeared to be nervous- looking over his shoulder, glancing around, and checking behind him.

The man, possibly unaware of the delivery driver still sitting in his vehicle, exits the building and enters a mini-van after removing his shirt. Thinking this was odd, the delivery driver entered the Frito Lay office only to discover the scene of a horror film.

He discovered the slumped over body of the regional manager, Thad Reynolds, sitting in a pool of his own blood. He called 911 and EMT's and police officers responded within minutes. However, it was too late. Thad Reynolds was dead before anyone arrived.

Ross Cavitt, a reporter at the scene, noted that Reynolds had been stabbed 19 times. Due to the nature of the stab wounds and the amount of blood, it was obvious to Cavitt that there had been a great struggle.

Thad's death sent shock through his community, but hit his church, the Hollywood Baptist, the hardest as Thad and his wife Michelle were well-known within the church community. In her early days, Michelle had been popular in high school and well respected within her community.

Thad, on the other hand, was a dedicated Christian and devoted father to his 4 children, as well as a loving husband to his wife, Michelle. As a young man, Thad had been heavily involved in sports and was popular at his high school.

"He could always make your day better" stated Julie Crumbley about her late friend Thad.

Michelle was a mother of 4 and a likeable person, according to Thad's close friend, Julie Crumbley.

Before becoming a mother, Michelle had worked as an administrative assistant, but had given the job up after giving birth to her first child in 1992. After the couple began to have children, the decision was made that Michelle would be a stay at home mom and raise their children.

In 1995, however, the couple's relationship took a turn for the worse and Michelle asked for a divorce. Thad's sister, Beverly Owners, claims that Michelle hadn't been happy just being a mother and a wife. It's been said that Michelle had made the following comment to a pastor at the couple's church: "You put your wife on a pedestal, but Thad never put me on a pedestal."

Thad agreed to the divorce, but regretted his decision as he didn't believe in divorce or broken homes. Undone by the divorce, Thad turned to his church for help. Two years after their divorce, the couple remarried, built a new home, and added more children to their family.

Thad's career began to flourish, after he was hired into the Frito Lay company where he was able to work his way to district manager. He also sang in the church's choir and served as a deacon, as well as helped other couples with marriage counseling.

"They appeared to be the most perfect family whenever you would see them" says Crumbley.

Thad's mother told Dateline that the couple had been called Barbie and Ken because of how well their life seemed to be going.

Both Michelle and Thad had a passion for children and worked with the church's youth group to put on shows, skits, and performances in various locations. They worked closely with the church's youth minister, Scott Harper and his wife, Paige. Thad and Scott became best friends and the families became joined at the hip. Paige and Michelle also became close, bonding over their stay at home lifestyles and busy husbands.

So, what went wrong? The answer to this was revealed only after a shocking truth involving Michelle and her best friend's husband came to light.

In 2004, Thad decided to become a minister, as he felt that God was calling to him to join the ministry. In June of that year, Michelle signed up to help the Harper family with a youth retreat, but called Paige shortly before they were set to leave and said that she had had a change of heart.

"She called me last minute and said that she was going to book her own room and was not going to room with me, because she needed her own time" says Paige, when asked about the phone call. This meant that Michelle would be the only chaperon who had her own private room.

"Michelle was distant. She wouldn't speak to me or look me in the eye" Paige says. Paige grew concerned and confronted her best friend. "I said "Michelle is there something wrong? Have I done something to offend you?" and she looked me in the eye and said no, I just want to be around people who are on fire for God."

As her husband prepared to become a minister, Michelle began to spend less time with Paige and more time with her husband, Scott.

"She would constantly be asking him for assistance. More and more she would ask him for help working with the children or how to do certain things with them. They began to email and communicate" says prosecutor, Leigh Patterson.

On Saturday, July 3rd, 2004, the Harper and Reynolds' met up for a long weekend celebration. The next day, a Sunday, the met up once again to attend church together. That day, the families met at a local park to play volleyball, gave snacks, and enjoy each other's company.

"I noticed Michelle being kind of flirtatious towards other men, asking somebody to help her throw a football and stuff like that." Paige says.

"She was a little bit too flirty...wanting other men to pay attention to her" agrees Patterson.

Despite Michelle's odd behavior at the picnic, she and her husband loaded up their children at the end of the evening and went home like nothing had happened.

The next morning Thad left for work before sunrise and while Michelle and the kids were still asleep. After only a few minutes at the office, a van pulled up outside of the office where Thad was working. The driver was Scott Harper, and within a few minutes, Thad would be dead on the floor of his office.

On July 5th, when Thad's body was discovered, the city of Rome, Georgia was thrown into chaos.

The first question on investigator's lips was who would launch a violent attack on the well-loved church deacon?

"There were wounds all over his body, including defensive wounds" says Patterson.

The only witness had been the delivery driver who had discovered Thad's body, but he had been unable to get a good look at Thad's attacker's face or the license plate of the van he had been driving.

Upon investigation of the scene, it became apparent to police that Thad had managed to wound his attacker. This was proved by a large amount of blood that was found by the office doorway- blood that matched up with the delivery driver's statement claiming that the unknown man stopped by the door before getting into his van and leaving the scene.

Also on the scene, police found the empty case for a hunting knife and a pair of glasses. The glasses also matched up with witness testimony, as the man was seen removing his shirt and in doing so, his glasses could have fallen off and been left behind in his haste to get away.

Scott Harper was called to help identify Thad's body and was one of the first people to learn of his death. Scott called his wife and upon hearing the news, Paige become worried about Michelle.

The Harpers drove to the Reynolds house to be with Michelle, however, upon arrival, they found that the church's head pastor was already there.

According to family and friends, Michelle has taken the news stoically.

"You would think that when we got there, Michelle would come and give us a hug or cry and she didn't" said Beverly Owens, surprised at how Michelle took the news.

Thad's mother also noticed Michelle's lack of outward emotion and was concerned by it.

"She had just bought a black dress about two weeks before and made the comment "whoever thought that I'd be using it for this.""

Meanwhile, back at the crime scene, investigators had begun to wonder about Thad's death. To them, it didn't appear to be a random attack and robbery situation, but seemed to have been calculated and planned, as Thad's murderer didn't take any of his money or anything that he had had on him. The reason behind the attack appeared to be one thing: to kill Thad Reynolds.

On the news that evening, a clue was unearthed as to who could have killed the deacon. Scott Roberts, a coworker of Scott Harper, had heard the news asking for leads and picked up the phone almost immediately.

Roberts called the police department and reported to the officials that his coworker, Scott Harper was both friends with Thad and drove a burgundy minivan like the one that had been witnessed leaving the crime scene.

Roberts was asked for a statement and while telling them what he knew, he alerted the police that Scott Harper had been having an affair with someone- information that he claimed he had stumbled upon without meaning to. Roberts worked with phonelines and was tasked with fixing them. A few weeks before the murder, he had tapped into a conversation to fix the phoneline and overheard Harper talking to a woman who wasn't his wife, Paige. He had also overheard that the woman's name was Michelle.

"They were flirting. Lover chit chat, if you will. Kind of reminded me of high school sweethearts" said Roberts in an interview with Dateline.

Officials ended their interview with Roberts by asking a simple question- did Harper wear glasses? Roberts had answered that, yes, Scott Harper did wear glasses.

This left police to wonder were the connections between the van, the glasses, and a possible affair all just coincidence? Or was there something sinister going on?

The Harpers were then brought in for official questioning, where Scott told investigators that he had hurt his hand at the gym, when he was asked why his hand was bandaged. This explained his hand but didn't explain why his glasses were missing.

Scott was released, despite police not believing his story. Paige was starting to doubt her husband, as well.

"When we left the station, I asked him if he knew anything about Thad's murder...about what was going on" Paige said "and he said "do you realize what you're asking me?""

Police obtained a warrant to search Scott's computer at the hospital that he worked at, in hopes of getting answers. They had a particular interest to look into Scott's emails, as they were saved on a public server and could be easily accessed.

It was found that a large portion of the emails were to and from Thad's wife, Michelle. At first, the emails were innocent- mostly consisting of routine topics such as the youth group that Michelle worked with at the church. Gradually, though, the emails became more personal and revealing in nature.

About a month before the death of her husband, the tone of the emails changed.

"She was coming onto him in the emails. Usually under the guise of I know I shouldn't feel this way" Patterson says, referring to Michelle and the emails that she sent to Scott "and he fell for it."

"The emails, especially toward the end, were very graphic and specific" said prosecutor Natalee Staats.

It wasn't clear from the emails when their affair became physical, however, records show that at the youth retreat in June, Scott had booked Michelle's room and stayed in it with her. Paige, although quiet about the whole thing, had noticed Scott get up and leave the room and noted that he didn't return until the next morning.

"He had gone down to Michelle's room and even though they were on a church trip with kids and his wife, and Michelle's daughter there as a participant, they had continued their affair" said Patterson.

Police combed over every detail of their emails, but couldn't decide whether Michelle had coaxed Scott into murdering her husband or not. According to Patterson, Michelle had been very careful with what she said and how she said it.

"Michelle never said "I need you to kill my husband" said Staats. However, she hinted at the idea by sayings things like "You'll have to live longer than Thad for us to be together because he'll never agree to divorce."

After Michelle had planted the idea in Scott's head, he had gone on to lookup poison and arsenic, as well an essay on how to commit the perfect murder Patterson reported.

On the evening of July 4th, hours before the murder would happen, the two exchanged a final round of emails.

"The night before, she tells him what Thad's schedule was going to be the next morning. Specific directions of where he was going to be" she also reports.

"Those were all glaring clues to the police that Michelle might have been involved in a conspiracy to murder her husband" said Staats, in agreeance with Patterson.

Scott had sent Michelle an email giving her an out. The email told Michelle to tell him if she had any hesitations, and that if she did, he wouldn't go through with it. Michelle replied that didn't have any hesitations and was ready for the event to take place.

Scott Harper was charged with murder on July 8th, 2004 after he turned himself in. He was charged with murder, felony murder, aggravated assault, and aggravated battery.

Authorities hoped that Scott would tie Michelle into the case, however, Scott was blinded by his feelings for her and was willing to protect her at all costs. He invoked the right to remain silent and didn't make another statement for or against Michelle's innocence.

Michelle was also arrested, as police had enough evidence from Michelle's own emails, that she had been involved.

"Once they figured it out, they decided pretty quickly that they had enough to charge her as well" said Michelle's attorney, Jim Berry.

An hour or so after Scott had turned himself in, Michelle was placed under arrest and brought into police custody and like her lover, Michelle refused to talk.

"Michelle was arrested as she came out of her attorney's office in downtown Rome" said Patterson.

"I had no clue. Everybody seemed happy" said Paige, who was shocked by the news that Michelle and Scott were in custody.

"Friends that they interacted with at the church didn't dream that the family pastor was having an affair with the deacon's wife" Patterson said.

The fact that Michelle and Scott could and would conspire to murder Thad Reynolds was unthinkable to the members of the church, who knew both people as being kind and good-hearted.

Scott Roberts, after hearing the news, took it upon himself to search the hospital where he and Scott worked for anything that police might have missed. He focused on the IT department's data center and more specifically, he focused on the tile floor. He was able to lift up a tile using a suction cup, and underneath, found the item that would be pinned as the murder weapon: a hunting knife. He also discovered a pile of bloody clothes.

In November, 4 months after Thad's murder, Michelle and Scott were summoned to the court room for a preliminary hearing to decide who would be tried first.

"The state gets to elect, by law, who to try first. We had elected to try her first" said Patterson. The decision to try Michelle first was a risk, as her case was the weaker of the two. Prosecutors knew that she hadn't bene the one to physically take Thad's life, however, they held her responsible for the murder.

"She was the person that made it happen" said Ross Cavitt "even though Scott Harper had the murder weapon in his hand, they could see that he was following orders from Michelle which made her ultimately responsible for the crime."

The emails, although suspicious, didn't pin Michelle to giving the orders, but prosecutors hoped that Harper would. They hoped that by presenting him with the evidence that was quickly stacking against him, they would be able to convince him to cut a deal and turn his back on Michelle.

Aside from the leverage of evidence that prosecutors had, the DA had written and notified the court that she would be seeking the death penalty for both Scott and Michelle.

"After the death of a fine young man, a father of four, to seek the death penalty wasn't that surprising" said Cavitt, in regard to the DA's email.

All that was left for prosecutors to do was wait and hope that Scott would cave.

"I had begged Scotty to do what was needed and to give up the information, and to tell the story of his involvement and Michelle's involvement" Paige told Dateline "and he would always tell me no, to just leave her out of this"

"He was smitten and head over heels in love with her" Cavitt said.

"I think that she couldn't have cared less about him. I think he was just the muscle behind the act" said Patterson, who was convinced that Michelle had simply used Harper's infatuation with her to get him to do her bidding.

Despite the prosecutor's hopes, Harper continued to clam up when it came to Michelle's involvement. It seemed that even the threat of the death penalty wasn't enough to get him to talk.

Years passed this way.

"Meetings with him resulted in nothing. He would not come forward" said Staats.

Finally, in the fall of 2008 and 4 years after both parties had been locked behind bars, Scott was ready to cooperate with prosecutors.

Scott's attorneys helped him decide on a deal and upon this conversation, it became to clear to everyone involved that Harper was still infatuated with Michelle as his concern for her took center stage. He would take a life sentence and plead guilty, as long as the death penalty was taken off of Michelle's case. He did, however, agree to testify at Michelle's trial.

"He effectively saved and betrayed her at the same time" said one of his attorneys.

In the court room on October 1st, 2008, Harper sat with prosecutors and told them his account of Thad's death.

"He told us that he still loved her and he was going to do anything in his power to minimize her involvement" said Patterson

"Michelle had basically said that Thad would not leave easily. He would fight for her and not give up on their marriage and that it would get ugly" said another of his attorneys "and he said that he could deal with ugly."

After this conversation, according to Scott, he had purchased the hunting knife and the next day, he had had lunch with Michelle. The two had parked and kissed in the back seat like a pair of teenagers, and it was during this time that Michelle had asked him if he had talked to her husband yet. When he told her that he hadn't, Michelle withdrew her affection and became cold and distant towards him.

Scott said that he had been afraid of losing her, so four days later he had woken up before dawn and driven to the Frito Lay distribution center with the intent to deal with Thad Reynolds.

As he entered the building, Thad had looked up and asked him what he was doing there. Scott Harper had replied with "I want what you got."

Harper's story was not enough to pin the murder on Michelle: it was only enough to charge her with adultery.

"All it would take was for one person on the jury to say that okay. Maybe Michelle really did think that Scott was just going to talk to her husband" Patterson said.

On January 13th, 2010, Michelle was brought back into court after 6 years of being in jail. The officials and attorneys present had been expecting for Harper to testify against Michelle, however, this did not happen. Michelle stood before the jury and plead guilty to voluntary manslaughter.

"Getting Scott Harper's statement was like pulling teeth and she didn't think we'd get it. That's the only reason that she plead guilty"

" She knew that she was responsible for the death, in some way, because of the affair and because of that she felt that she should plead guilty to something" said Scott's attorney.

At the hearing that day, Thad's mother asked Michelle why her son had had to die for this.

"There was no response" said Thad's mother, Kittie Walker, "her eyes were just cold. No remorse, no feelings, nothing."

"She knew that Thad would not have let her take the kids away" said Beverly Owens "and she knew that that was the only way to get him out of the picture"

In the end, she was sentenced to 20 years behind bars, with credit being given to the time she had already served in county jail. Until her release, Michelle is unable to see her children and will lose custody of them.

According to Scott Roberts, there were people who upon hearing her sentencing, didn't feel as if justice had been served.

"I would have liked to see Michelle get a lot more time for it. I would have liked to see her life in prison" said Kittie Walker.

Many people in Rome, Georgia agreed that although Scott had wielded the knife, Michelle was the villain behind the plot.

"We're in a religious town and I think that many people believed that Scotty had been manipulated by her and that she was the devil incarnate" said Jim Berry.

Despite the tension and hard feelings, Paige Harper was visibly shaken by the case.

"Scott and Michelle were the two most important people in my life other than my kids, so for this to happen...it really makes me wonder how well I know people" she said.

In the aftermath of the murder, Thad's mother got custody of the kids and Paige divorced her husband in 2005. Despite writing letters in the early days of their sentences, Michelle and Scott have stopped communicating.

Within recent years, Michelle has written to officials asking why she isn't allowed to see her children.

"We do it all the time with adults- no contact with whomever. That's not anything new. That's a standard law order in nearly every murder case I've had, even if they're in the same family" responded Patterson, who also stated that Michelle is well aware of this order as it was part of her plea deal back in January of 2010.

Judge J. Bryant Durham, who had found Michelle guilty in years prior, mentioned that once her children turn 18 they can visit her in prison. Currently, this means that Michelle's eldest daughter, 22-year old Alisan and her infant grandchild can visit her in prison whenever they wish.

"Like it or not, if she decides to go over there every day, I don't think that can be stopped" Durham told Patterson.

The intent of the order was to restrict visitation until Michelle was released, however, due to lack of specifics and bad wording, the age of visitation remains 18.

There's no question that a good man died for less than good reasons, but there are still questions in the minds of his family and friends. Why had it happened? Had death really been Michelle's only option? It's up for speculation and, unfortunately, no one will ever know for sure.

KILLING THE WRONG MAN : THE TRUE STORY OF LEE ANN REIDEL

132

ANITA MURDOCK

What could lead a normal middle class woman to be accused of killing an innocent man? This is the story of convicted murderer Lee Ann Reidel.

Early Years

Lee Ann Reidel, then Lee Ann Armanini, was born in the summer of 1967. Her childhood was very normal. She was the second of four children, to parents David and Pat Armanini. The family lived in a middle class, suburban area in Long Island, New York. Things went well for a few years; they went on regular vacations and spent the holidays together, life was good.

It was when Lee Ann turned 11 that things started to go wrong. Her parents divorced. Pat Armanini, Lee Ann's mother, moved to Florida to live with a new female lover. Lee Ann was left behind in New York. From that point she was raised by her father, David Armanini, who later remarried. Unsurprisingly, these difficult circumstances seemed to have a negative effect on Lee Ann's life and she entered a downward spiral.

Her teenage years were troubled, culminating in a failed marriage at the young age of 19. As a result of this marriage Lee Ann had her first child, a son named Christopher. Lee Ann raised Christopher alone and had the typical struggles of a young, single mother. The main worry was money; some claim that financial insecurities during this period of Lee Ann's life affected her later actions. However, despite some tough times, David Armanini, Lee Ann's father, claims that she was a responsible mother, who put the needs of her son first.

Family Life

The following years passed without incident. Lee Ann didn't have another serious boyfriend until she met Paul Reidel in 1998. The pair met at a Long Island gym where Lee Ann had started working out. They quickly fell in love. Friends of Lee Ann claim that she was very happy. She liked Paul Reidel because he was a strong, muscly man who could protect her, but he also had a gentle nature. The relationship progressed quickly, and soon they were engaged. Cathy Armanini, Lee Ann's stepmother, stated that the family were very pleased when they discovered that the pair had plans to marry.

Paul Reidel had a difficult past – he spent several years in prison on drug dealing charges when he was 19. However, he had since reformed and become a very ambitious man. He opened a business named Dolphin Fitness Club, with his best friend, Alex Algeri. Dolphin Fitness Club in Amityville, New York, was a popular 24 hour gym for weightlifters. The business was thriving and Paul was doing very well financially. Lee Ann appreciated her new lifestyle – she had gone from being a struggling single mother, to the partner of a rich business owner.

Lee Ann and Paul had a church wedding in July 1998. The wedding was quite a lavish display, with impressive decorations and catering. Guests described it as a beautiful fairy tale wedding. No one would ever have predicted the terrible events that were soon to follow.

Marriage Troubles

Not long after they were married, Lee Ann discovered that she was pregnant with her second child. Again, family members were delighted. From the outside everything seemed perfect. However, the stress of owning a 24 hour business and the prospect of being a father was starting to get to Paul. He had started using drugs again and quickly became addicted to crack cocaine.

Pat Armanini, Lee Ann's mother, claims that Lee Ann confided in her about Reidel's drug use and that she was very distressed by it. A number of incidents took place involving Lee Ann driving around during the night, trying to locate Paul and bring him back home. Pat Armanini stated that on one occasion Lee Ann even followed him to the location of a drug deal in order to prevent it from happening. This all happened while Lee Ann was heavily pregnant. Lee Ann wanted to preserve their relationship and help Paul get off drugs. Her mother believes that she thought the new baby would fix things between them, and be the wake-up call that Paul needed to stop taking crack cocaine.

For a short time, this did seem to be the case. Paul became very excited about the idea of having a child, especially when he found out it was a boy. When the child was born, they called him Nicholas. Paul asked his best friend and business partner, Alex Algeri, to be Nicholas' godfather. Algeri happily agreed.

However, despite a happy period, Paul Reidel's drugs habits remained. He continued to use crack cocaine regularly. Lee Ann would apparently find needles and vials around the house, and feared that their small child would end up getting injured or worse. In July 2000, things came to ahead and Paul returned home from work one night to find that Lee Ann, his new born baby and stepson, were gone. Also missing was a large amount of money and possessions from the house. Lee Ann had fled to her mother's place in Florida with the children, taking $120000 with her.

Losing his family seemed to be the wake-up call that Paul Reidel needed. He was afraid that he would no longer be able to see his son. Reidel hired a lawyer to help fight for shared custody of Nicholas and he wanted Lee Ann and the baby to come back to New York while they waited for a custody decision. Paul stated that he wanted to be part of Nicholas' life, and he couldn't do that from so far away. Ultimately though, Reidel did not want his family to fall apart and he spent the next four months trying to reconcile with his wife. He made many promises to Lee Ann during this time. Most importantly, Reidel agreed to go to rehab and ditch his cocaine habit.

Lee Ann and the children eventually returned to Long Island in December 2000. It seemed like the two were trying to sort out their marriage and wanted to try again. Everyone believed that they had gotten over the difficult drugs issues and were now on the path towards happy family life once more. Paul was pleased, he was able to stay in the area of his business, and see his wife and son every day. However, not all was as it seemed and Lee Ann's motivations for returning to Long Island would later be called into question.

The Murder

One month later on the 17th January 2001, an unbelievable act of violence took place. Alex Algeri was shot in the face and killed outside the Dolphin Fitness Club. Gym members and the local community of Amityville were shocked; it was obviously a cold blooded murder.

Like any typical January in New York, the weather was very cold and there was a covering of snow on the ground. It was 7.20 in the evening and already dark. It was Paul Reidel's night off; Alex Algeri was covering the late shift at the gym. During what had so far been a perfectly normal evening, Alex popped out to get a CD from his car for one of the regular aerobics classes. He exited the building through the backdoor. The car park was not well lit and would have been very dark. He went round to the passenger side of the car to collect the CD from the glove compartment. Suddenly, a man jumped out of another vehicle parked nearby. As Algeri turned around, the man shot him several times in the face and neck.

Alex Algeri made it back into the gym trying to get help, but quickly collapsed and was dead before he arrived at hospital.

There was chaos. No one could understand why anyone would want Alex Algeri dead. The consensus was that Algeri was a friendly, popular individual who didn't have any known enemies. For a long time, the police had no leads in their investigation into the murder and people began to wonder if Algeri was really the intended victim.

Rumours spread that perhaps the killer had meant to shoot Paul Reidel instead. After all, Paul was the one with the criminal background. He had taken and dealt drugs for many years, and could have gotten involved with the wrong person. Maybe he had drug related debts, or someone was jealous of his flashy lifestyle. However, at this point there was no evidence that this was the case.

Lee Ann seemed to become panicked after Algeri's funeral. She apparently started asking Paul if it was supposed to be him, and what if she and the baby had been there – what if someone came to their house. Lee Ann convinced Paul that they might be in danger in New York, and that the family should move back to Florida.

Running Away

In 2001, the family did just this. Reidel, Lee Ann and the two children, Christopher and Nicholas, moved back to Florida permanently. Reidel was now the sole owner of the Dolphin Fitness Club and he wanted to remain in charge of the Long Island business. He decided to try and run things from Florida, flying out on regular business trips to check how everything was going. Lee Ann and Paul had plans to build a house for them and their two children in Florida. According to Lee Ann's friend, Mary Hanrahan, Lee Ann and Reidel were both very positive about the move. Reidel apparently spoke excitedly about their plans to build a property and yet again, everything appeared to be going fine for them.

The police in Long Island still had a murder investigation with no leads. Months passed without any new information on the case.

On one of Paul's many business trips to New York he received some unpleasant news from a relative. His relative claimed that every time Paul went out of town, a man went to see Lee Ann at the husband and wife's apartment in Florida. The suspicion was that Lee Ann was involved in an affair.

Reidel quickly dismissed the stories about Lee Ann being unfaithful. He believed that their relationship was stronger than ever because Lee Ann was pregnant again. He even told his relatives that the couple planned to call their new baby Paul, after him. Perhaps some family members had their doubts, but for several months everything went smoothly and Lee Ann and Reidel seemed content together.

A Lead

However, all that was about to change. In November 2001 police arrested a drug dealer in New York, named Michael Hubbard. Hubbard tipped off police that Ralph Salierno and Scott Paget from Florida were involved in the murder of Alex Algeri. Hubbard was trying to help the police and give them the impression that he was cooperating in the hope that his own drug dealing convictions would be dropped.

Police quickly brought in Salierno and Paget for questioning. From the very beginning Paget claimed that Salierno was the one who actually committed the murder and fired the gun at Algeri. Paget stated that he was just the driver. Salierno feigned ignorance about the murder for a while, but when he discovered that Paget had pointed the finger at him, he decided to offer his own rundown of events. In Salierno's story, Lee Ann was the one who came up with the plan to commit a murder, and Salierno was merely trying to follow her instructions.

Salierno confirmed that he and Lee Ann had been having an affair since the first time she moved to Florida in July 2000. Lee Ann's own mother, Pat Armanini, had introduced them, with the idea that Salierno could protect Lee Ann if Paul Reidel ever came to Florida and tried to take baby Nicholas. However, the relationship had developed into something much more. The two had fallen in love and kept seeing each other even when Lee Ann and Reidel were supposedly back together. Salierno claimed that Lee Ann had given him instructions to go to New York and kill Paul Reidel, offering him a potential payment of $100000. Salierno said that the killing of Alex Algeri was a case of mistaken identity.

Paul Reidel and Alex Algeri did not look dissimilar; they were both very strong, muscular men and had similar features. Obviously, they shared the same work place and even drove the same type of car. The murder had also taken place in the poorly lit gym carpark on a dark January evening. A case of mistaken identity did not seem impossible to police. Salierno's story was further backed up when he revealed that he was the father of Lee Ann's third child. This proved to be true, meaning that Lee Ann and Salierno had continued to see each other even after Alex Algeri's murder. So far, Salierno's version of events appeared to be adding up.

After Salierno admitted to killing Alex Algeri, Lee Ann confessed that she had indeed been having an affair with Salierno. The new baby, named Zachary, was his. However, she strongly denied that she had any part in planning her husband's murder. Lee Ann claimed that Salierno must have committed the murder in a fit of jealousy over the fact that the husband and wife appeared to be reconciling, and that Algeri was simply in the wrong place at the wrong time. Lee Ann also said that she had continued the affair with Salierno after Alex Algeri's death because her husband had changed – he was withdrawn and paranoid. She maintained that she had no idea that Salierno was the one who killed Algeri.

The police were put in a difficult situation – they were faced with numerous conflicting stories and very little physical evidence. They concluded that the only option was to let the case go to court and see what the outcome would be. In March 2003 Lee Ann Reidel was also arrested for the murder of Alex Algeri, it was decided that she and Salierno would be co-defendants.

The Trial

In March 2004, Lee Ann and Salierno were tried in the same room at Suffolk County courthouse, and faced the same prosecutors, but the outcome would be decided by two different juries. This is quite an unusual set up. The pair faced several charges including first degree murder, second degree murder and conspiracy to commit murder.

The prosecutor was Assistant District Attorney Denise Merrifield. Merrifield began by establishing that the intended victim was in fact, Paul Reidel, not Alex Algeri. Salierno confirmed this in his admission. The real question was did Salierno act alone, or was he acting on the instruction of Lee Ann?

Many witnesses were called upon during the trial. There was no physical evidence of Lee Ann's involvement so the prosecution relied heavily on the testimony of these witnesses. One notable testimony was from Lee Ann's mother's former lover, Elizabeth Russo. Russo claimed that she and Lee Ann's mother had initially introduced Lee Ann and Salierno with the intention of providing protection to Lee Ann. Salierno was told that if Paul Reidel came to Florida Salierno should threaten him and break his legs. This account suggested that Lee Ann was open to violent acts towards Paul Reidel. Russo clearly implied that she believed Lee Ann was capable of giving the instruction to Salierno to commit murder. Russo's account was particularly important for the prosecution because, unlike most of the other witnesses they called, she was not a criminal.

Scott Paget had already admitted that he drove Salierno back and forth to Long Island, New York on the night of the murder. Paget said that Salierno paid him $3000 dollars to drive the getaway car. He received a lower sentence of 18 years for cooperation with police. He also testified against Lee Ann – though the defence maintained that he could have simply been doing this in order to help his own case. Paget testified that Lee Ann instructed Salierno to kill Reidel. He said that Lee Ann gave Salierno a photograph of Reidel and told him the address of the Dolphin Fitness Club. Although this was a damning testimony, the defence tried to argue that Paget was not a reliable witness due to his own conviction and involvement in the case.

However, Lee Ann's case was damaged further when Michael Paglianti, a Florida drug dealer, was called to give his testimony. He said that he had been present when Lee Ann and Salierno met and discussed breaking Paul Reidel's legs. He also claimed that he had heard Lee Ann say that she wanted Reidel dead. Paglianti corroborated Paget's story by saying that he saw Lee Ann give a photograph of Reidel to Salierno. Finally, Paglianti testified that after the night of the murder and Algeri's funeral, Lee Ann verbally abused Salierno for killing the wrong guy.

Having heard from numerous witnesses, Lee Ann's case was not looking good. However, the defence pointed out that most of the witnesses were criminals and there was still no physical evidence of Lee Ann's guilt. There were some discrepancies with the car that Salierno and Paget drove to Long Island, with no record of who paid for the car, or where they rented it from. Lee Ann's attorney, Bruce Barket, questioned why Salierno had killed the wrong man. Surely, if he was acting on Lee Ann's instruction, he would have known that it was Reidel's night off and that Algeri was working at the club that night.

There was still the question of why Lee Ann would want her husband dead. The prosecution had a simple answer for this – money. They claimed that Lee Ann wanted Paul Reidel out of the picture so that she could start a new life with Salierno whilst living comfortably on Reidel's savings.

The prosecution, Denise Merrifield, believed that Lee Ann already started developing the plan to murder Reidel the first time she was in Florida in July 2000. Merrifield suggested that Lee Ann knew that if the husband and wife remained separated when Reidel was killed, she would be a number one suspect. Merrifield said that Lee Ann then pretended to reconcile with Reidel and moved back to New York, all whilst plotting his murder with Salierno. Her plan was to act like the grieving widow after his death, in order to seem innocent. As Reidel's wife, his fortune would be left to her and she would let some time pass before quietly moving back to Florida to be with Salierno.

Of course, the defence disputed this story. Defence attorney Bruce Barket maintained that Salierno went to New York in a fit of rage upon seeing that Lee Ann and Reidel were back together. Barket stated that Salierno's actions were irrational and not well planned; this is how he ended up shooting the wrong person. According to the defence, Lee Ann was oblivious to the fact that Salierno had killed Algeri and that her only wrong doing was the ongoing affair with Salierno.

In the end, it seemed like the decision could go either way for Lee Ann.

The Decision

The jury deciding the fate of Salierno returned to the court room in just four hours. He was found guilty of first degree murder and Judge Louis Ohlig sentenced him to life in prison with no parole.

Lee Ann's jury took longer to reach a decision. Her defence attorney believed that this was a good sign for her case. However, after four long days, the jury found her guilty too. Lee Ann was held equally responsible for the death of Alex Algeri. On the 28th April 2004, she was sentenced to twenty five years to life. The prosecution did not ask for life without parole for Lee Ann. They did not give any comment on why this was, which was unusual because the judge even stated that he would have happily given a longer sentence to Lee Ann had the prosecution asked for it.

Prosecutor Merrifield told the judge that "Justice has been served here, your honour. She, because of her own greed and evil heart, wanted her husband dead. This defendant is the most self-absorbed defendant I have ever prosecuted."

Bruce Barket, Lee Ann's defence attorney, was very upset by the outcome of the case. This is clear from his response to the decision: "I respect the Jury system. I respect the Jury process. I strongly disagree with the verdict."

Although Lee Ann's attorney claims to respect the Jury process, there has been some criticism of the way the case was handled in court. Some believe that the fact that Lee Ann and Salierno were tried in the same room was actually damaging to Lee Ann's case. The psychology of seeing the pair together, with the knowledge that they had an ongoing affair and a child together, could have affected the Jury's decision. The idea that Lee Ann was guilty of something was already in the minds of the Jury members, perhaps they found it hard to make an objective decision on Lee Ann's guilt in relation to the murder itself.

There was also the fact that the unintended victim of the murder was someone completely innocent and well liked. This caused wide spread anger, even those who did not know Alex Algeri felt that it was a real tragedy and an injustice. People were calling for the death penalty, though this was not requested by the prosecution. The high levels of emotion and anger surrounding the case could also have impacted on the Jury's decision making. It's hard to say if the reaction would have been the same if Reidel had been the one killed. It is possible that it would have been easier for the defence to portray Reidel as someone involved in a criminal lifestyle and Lee Ann as a fearful wife, desperate to escape his control. As Algeri was the victim, the Judge potentially felt a lot of pressure to dish out harsh sentences in an attempt to restore justice.

Alex Algeri was only 32 when he was murdered. His sister, Christie Stoll, told the judge "our brother is gone and the hole in our hearts will never be filled because of [Lee Ann's] greed and hatred of her husband. Even though Lee Ann Reidel wasn't there on the night of January 17th 2001, she just as well might have been. Lee Ann Reidel is just as guilty as Ralph Salierno." After the trial Algeri's father, Salvatore Algeri, said that "justice has been served completely."

Despite the defence claiming no evidence, and the issue raised about the nature of the trial, the widely held opinion is that justice was done and that Lee Ann was guilty for her part in Alex Algeri's murder.

Zachary, Lee Ann's third child, fathered by Salierno, is living with Lee Ann's sister in Long Island. Lee Ann and Reidel's son Nicholas is living with Reidel and no longer has any contact with his mother. Paul Reidel gave an insightful interview on the extremely popular talk show, Larry King live. He said that Lee Ann wanted him dead because she knew he would never stop fighting for access to their son. When asked if he felt lucky to have avoided murder, Reidel said "I don't feel lucky, because I would have took that walk. I would have never asked him to do it, and whatever happened, that's a burden I'll always carry." Reidel explained that his life is in order and his ongoing focus is raising his son. "I feel like I have a severe obligation to be a good man and do the right thing by my son because I feel like I owe that to Alex". King also asked Reidel what his feelings were towards Lee Ann, Reidel said that he did not hate her, but that he was confused and that he felt that she deserved the prison sentence.

Salierno is currently serving his sentence at Attica Correctional Facility in New York. Lee Ann is at Bedford Hills Correctional Facility also in New York. So far, her attempts to appeal have been unsuccessful.

KILL HIM JILL

Sarah Thompson

For some, gambling is a special treat - a past-time for birthdays, anniversaries and celebrations. It can be a bonding experience that brings everyone together through either luck, or misfortune. For others, gambling becomes an addiction, where they are willing to lie, cheat and steal in order to get their fix. For the lucky few, gambling can become a lifestyle. This lifestyle is often fraught with drugs, danger, embezzlement, lies and fraud. Like many of the stories that have come before them, the story of Bill Gustafik and Jill Rockcastle is one that would make any big-screenwriter proud. When you put in all the ingredients of drugs, grand theft, a professional poker player, a murder and an attempt at suicide, you get something that sounds so surreal, no one could have lived through it.

The truth is, Jill Rockcastle did live through it - but her husband, tragically, did not. While one's heart may feel the instinctive pull to go out to Jill, the reality is much worse. The story of Bill and Jill is set in Las Vegas, where gambling, drugs and danger go hand-in-hand. In the early morning hours of April 13th in 2007, police received an anonymous tip about a dead body on the 23rd floor of a condominium building. This was only the beginning of a web that would slowly begin to unravel, and make it clear that the story of Jill Rockcastle is almost indistinguishable from the story of Bill Gustafik - you cannot tell one story without the other. They're inseparable, even after death.

Jill Rockcastle and Bill Gustafik seemed like a couple who couldn't be happier. Jill and Bill met not long after Bill had divorced his previous wife in 2000. He had also graduated from chiropractor's school - a long way off from his eventual calling as a professional poker player. Meanwhile, Jill worked in the mortgage business, refinancing people's homes for them. It made her enough money to be independent and happy. Bill and Jill met in the months following his divorce, and hit it off as friends quite well. They started as friends, and stayed this way for about two years. But their relationship started to grow and build quite quickly. They eventually got married in 2005, but their relationship was one of devotion and obsession long before that. It was built on lies, secrets, fraud, and a desire to become better and more fabulous than the lives that they were currently leading.

Their relationship worked because, by Jill's own words, they discovered that they were able to get whatever they wanted out of people. However, their reasons were far different. Jill was able to manipulate the people around her because of what she described as "a need to survive." On the other hand, Bill did what he did out of, what Jill described as, "a need to conquer." In stark contrast to Jill's desires, Bill wanted to to be the most superior and successful person to walk into a room.

Their driving desires were far different, but they worked together all the same. Two master manipulators joined together to form a power couple that would lead them both to their eventual ends. Despite his good life, Bill wanted more. He longed to be one of the richest, most powerful people in the room when he walked in, and Jill was able to help him get it. Jill's inheritance money and her job as a refinancing for mortgages allowed her to live the lavish lifestyle that her partner craved. Even in the beginning of their relationship, the two worked together to manipulate whatever system was set up against them.

The Bill and Jill began their partnership in crime not long after they got together. Bill was going through a custody evaluation with his ex-wife. Both Bill and his ex-wife had been in a custody battle over their nine year old daughter for some time, perhaps all the time that Bill and Jill had known one another. Bill's child support payments would have been $4,000 given to his wife - but Bill asked Jill to re-worked his income in the books so that it looked as if he was being paid less than he actually was. Jill had software that was used to prepare your own tax returns. She showed him that she could alter the returns, and that brought bill out of the rage that had consumed him over the possibility of giving his ex-wife four grand in child support. Jill's solution was a savior - together, Bill and Jill worked their magic to cut down Bill's earnings.

Or was it magic? Jill's life story with Bill was left behind in a ten-page suicide note. While Jill Rockcastle never managed to go through with the planned attempt, the note leaves behind sordid and intimate details of their lives. The beginning of their schemes apparently started with a threat. In her note, Jill describes the first arrangement together, shedding more light on the custody scheme. At first, Jill refused Bill's request to arrange his income so that it looked as if he were earning less than he actually was. But then, Bill began to threaten her. A few days before the court hearing, Jill held the phone against her ear, listening to Bill bellow at her from the other end - screaming about how badly he needed her to do this for him. Like many women in her position, the threats and shouting worked, and Jill conceded to the plan.

And that plan also worked. The morning of the court hearing, Jill gave in and fixed the tax return documents to reflect a much lower income that Bill was truly earning. Their first scheme allowed for Bill to pay only $1,800 in child support - less than half of the proposed amount. In her 10 page letter, Jill wrote, "We began living without rules and not afraid of consequence." After all, what an exhilarating moment - to break the law and get away with it. It's no wonder that Jill and Bill became addicted to the thrill of it all. Not to mention, the money that came rolling in with it.

Bill Gustafik eventually opened up his own office in Antioch. Jill worked there with him, though her job behind the scenes was a bit different. She fixed the books in order to subtly increase the profit made between them. Jill was also instructed by Bill to finance real estate deals for some of the patients that came into Bill's chiropractor's office, in order for the income to go directly to Jill. The money that they made together was more than enough - and at the same time, it was nowhere near enough.

While Bill had his own talents when it came to these schemes, it was Jill who was the mastermind. In 2004, Bill took over one of this offices in Hayward, becoming the owner. Jill was the one who helped him purchase the entire building, and Jill was the one who helped him buy the building as an LLC, so that the purchase would have no effect on his personal credit. Meanwhile, Bill used his own talents in scamming his patients. Person after person, Bill would overcharge and over treat his patients in order to get as much money as possible. While Bill was doing this, it was Jill who was working behind the scenes for him - fixing his books, making sure that Bill was getting even more money than he worked for.

Jill had her own schemes, too. Independent of Bill, Jill Rockcastle worked deals, financing larger homes with large mortgages. On each home, Jill would get 2% or more on each one - that meant on a deal that was $700,000, Jill would take home $14,000. This allowed Jill to work less than Bill. In fact, she only worked once or twice a month. Even $8,000 was more than Jill usually spent in a month. While she was content with their level of riches, Bill wasn't. He wanted more, and with Jill at his side, he was determined to get it.

Bill wanted more of of life - even more than his 7 am to 7 pm lifestyle of scamming patients and fixed books was giving him. Bill began to obsess over getting on television. He wanted to play poker, and he wanted to do so on TV. Despite his already lavish lifestyle, Bill wanted more than just that. He wanted global recognition. Jill went along with it - after all, she had the time, and she has the devotion to Bill.

The note that had been left behind, written in Jill's own words, describes how it was around this time that the two of them went off to Las Vegas together - a city full of glittery lights, casinos, gambling, and eventual devastation. It was in October of 2004 that Jill followed Bill to Las Vegas. As she puts it, their move to Las Vegas was "the beginning of the con." Bill began to live the lifestyle that he believed he deserved - one that was lavish, with extravagant spending. It was Jill who continued to make it all possible, and Jill who continued to watch on. She helped him buy two houses, and get his extravagant car. Everything that Bill had and wanted was because of Jill. Without Jill Rockcastle, he would still be stuck, paying the $4,000 of child support to his ex wife. Bill's desire to be rich in a visible way left Jill vying to make herself worthy of him - she got plastic surgery, enhancing herself to look just like another one of Bill Gustafik glittering trophies.

Jill Rockcastle's letter reveals an even darker side of Bill - one that she, alone, was privy to. There was a time, undisclosed by the note, simply "two years ago", when Jill and Bill had Bill's daughter with them during Christmas time. Jill exposes the man Bill had been. All the time that they had been together, Jill had helped fix everything so that Bill would not have to pay the proposed amount to his ex-wife for child support. Despite Jill's abilities, Bill still wanted to problem gone once and for all. Jill described, in a note to Bill's ex wife, in a chilling lack of detail, that Bill had attempted to have his ex-wife and his ex mother in law killed.

An attempted assassination that didn't go through - the man had taken the money and bolted, leaving Bill both without his money, and Jill with the lasting impression of the lengths that Bill would go to. In Jill's note, she described she believed the Bill felt no love. In her note,

Jill says, "He knew deep down that he could not care for someone. [...] he didn't feel love. [...] he didn't feel compassion." This was the man that Jill had been living with for so long. If this man would attempt to put a hit out on his ex wife, there's no telling what he would do to Jill if she didn't continue to fund the lifestyle to which Bill was becoming accustomed.

Jill Rockcastle and Bill Gustafik were living a life that Jill's note described as "the life of fake millionaires". In Las Vegas, Bill finally began to play poker just as he had been obsessing over. The problem arose that Bill wasn't very good. In fact, his first night playing saw that Bill lost nearly ten thousand dollars. Their life together in Las Vegas wasn't everything that it seemed. The money was running out. Together, they were going broke. Their schemes continued on, the con growing and growing, until neither of them had complete control over what they were doing. The new schemes began with getting people to give Jill money. After all, Bill was still struggling with his ex-wife's custody battle. If he obtained more money, it would be scrutinized for child support. So it was Jill who ran the scams, and Jill who brought in the money.

The newest scam to get money was selling fake real estate. Jill allowed the cognitive dissonance get the better of her. Even some of the people who were supposedly their friends fell victim to Bill and Jill - there was nothing and no one that they couldn't con when they put their heads together. All the while, Jill told herself that she was helping out. Even if what they were doing was wrong, Jill was devoted to Bill. She loved him, and she wanted to help him. How could she say no? After all, they had left their lives behind, left behind Bill's doctor's offices, all for the bright light and excitements of Las Vegas. Bill wanted to be a high roller, and for a short while, Jill was rich. She allowed herself to block out the things that they were doing. In her letter, she says, "That's how I lived with my sick self."

But Bill was spending money faster than Jill could bring it it. He began to do drugs, and Jill would watch, dispassionate, as Bill would do lines of cocaine and play online poker. They were running out of money faster than Jill could replenish it. He would play a poker tournament and lose upwards of $15,000. Jill was a gambler as well, but she was better at it than Bill. She wasn't a poker player - rather her game of choice was Roulette. Jill could easily win thousands upon thousands of dollars. But, as quickly as Jill won $20,000 at Roulette, Bill would take it again. She would barely have time to text him of her winnings before he would come from the poker room, take it, and lose it again.

Jill began to squirrel money away. She knew that there was no possible way that they could keep going on like this. She kept money hidden from Bill, giving it to her children - both grown, at the time - if they ever needed it. Bill was beginning to get frustrated and desperate. Jill tucked away her money, and pulled several more scams that kept Bill in earnings to spend and lose. It was Jill who went to the bank to deposit money in order to keep their bills paid while Bill continued hemorrhage winnings. It was always Jill who had to deposit the money. Every once in awhile, Bill would give her cash and have her deposit it in the bank. The money had to look as if it were coming from Jill, least Bill's ex-wife become aware that Bill was skimming on his custody payments.

Jill was starting to breakdown. Her life had been reduced to running scams, telling lies, and bowing to Bill's whims. Jill knew that she had to stop Bill somehow. In her ten page suicide note, Jill describes, "I"m going to skip so many things in an effort to shorten this but my life was a constant hell for the last year. I'm going to skip all the lawsuits [...] All the tax notices. All the bounced checks. All the drugs." It was this hell that drove Jill to feeling as if she was the only one who was able to put a stop to Bill. She made phone calls to friends and other connections, feeling an ever overwhelming desperation. Jill even made a call to her attorney, desperate for someone to help her and get her out of the situation - her attorney only told her that Bill was addicted to gambling, and that the only thing to do is to wait until he has nothing left. But waiting was not something that Jill could, or would, do.

Jill took it into her own hands to stop bill, after having gone to the doctor and found out that the stress of the situation has started to give her shingles. At 7:30 in the evening, police received a call from an anonymous person, telling them of a dead body. When police investigators arrived, they wound Bill Gustafik dead. His body was in the master bedroom, and a kitchen knife was stashed away in the trash bin. The police had very little contention among them about who the suspect could be. Upon first glancing at the scene of the crime, they immediately suspected Jill Rockcastle.

The crime was quick. For Jill Rockcastle, killing her husband was not a drawn out plan, with weeks in the making. Nor was Bill Gustafik's death one that caused the police to go on a chase for their suspect. The night before what Jill called "the incident", the couple got into an argument - like most of the arguments in these days, it was about money. The day previous, Bill was leaving for the Bellagio Hotel, located in Las Vegas. He wanted Jill to pay his buy-ins for a poker tournament, and he wanted her to bring $30,000 for him to use. But Jill didn't bring the money. Either she couldn't get it, or she refused to. When she got to their shared Las Vegas condo, the couple began to argue. But the fight didn't end there. After going to sleep angry, Bill and Jill awoke in the morning to continue the same argument. Bill continued to demand Jill to give him money that he could play with. This time, Bill demanded $7,500 from her. Still, she refused.

Bill's aggression began to build. Jill's fears were starting to become realized. He was threatening to kill her, along with her ex wife. It was then that Jill made an attempt to leave. As she went to leave, Bill physically blocked her with his body. He forced her back from the door and into the kitchen. Jill grabbed a knife from the kitchen to defend herself, fearing for her life. The note described how Jill was afraid that

Bill would kill her, just as he had said that he would do. She couldn't escape him, though. He simply kept coming for her, and Jill did what she knew would stop Bill once and for all. She swing the knife into his chest, holding the weapon with both hands. When he went down, Jill still had the knife in her hands. In her own words, Jill says she "just snapped".

Jill stabbed him over fifteen times. Just like that, Bill was gone. There was no grand plan. After years of scamming, scheming, lying and cheating, Jill was done. The story of Bill and Jill ends the way so many women's stories have ended - a dead husband, a knife in their hands, years of fear and abuse behind them. While the story leading up to Bill's death involved so many lies, and so many cons, the story of his death is an anticlimactic one. A death that Bill wouldn't have been proud of - the only thing that made him notable in death was the same that made him notable in life: his wife, Jill. And though Bill had gone out as many men do, stabbed and left for dead, it was Jill Rockcastle that made sure everyone would remember his name, and her own.

After he was dead, Jill cleaned up after herself, cleaned herself up, and fled from the condo. Just like that, Bill Gustafik was dead and Jill Rockcastle was on the run. She had stopped him, just as she knew that she had to do. It was then that Jill Rockcastle disappeared, and on the Monday after Bill Gustafik's death, Jill Rockcastle sent an email to her friends, family and various business partners. The email included ten pages of a suicide note. The note goes in depth on all of Jill's struggles throughout her time of having known Bill, and all of the things that had happened to her. The note describes Bill's struggles with his gambling addiction, and many of the scams and schemes that they had performed today. It was, essentially, ten pages of confessions, implicating herself in all of the things that she and Bill had done together. But, it was always a note to tell everyone goodbye.

In her email, Jill wrote: "This is my final statement done to help all the people affected by my actions [...] and the results of whatever happen to them in our aftermath. I'm writing this so that each person that receives it will identify with the time period in which your experience occurred with him and I and can have some of the why [...] answered. I am not trying in anyway to justify a single thing in here. I am not looking to clear my name or actions. I have already done the most final things possible to stop us from hurting anyone else."

The email was a suicide note, one that was meant to tell everyone that nothing that she and Bill had done would ever touch them again. She alludes here to Bill's death, and to what she had planned to do in order to "stop us" from continuing on how she had been.

Of course, police investigators couldn't let Jill Rockcastle get away with what she had done by allowing her to kill herself. An attempt to find Jill where she had fled was made, first by searching her home in San Ramon that she had kept with Bill. The Las Vegas police called the San Ramon police and urged them to go to the home that Jill and Bill had owned together in San Ramon, in order to arrest her or take her to the hospital, depending on how far she had gone through with her plan to end her life.

However, police investigators were shocked to find that Jill Rockcastle was not in her home in San Ramon. When the police broke down her door, there was no one. Another anonymous call was given to the Las Vegas police, this time urging them on to another location, this time in San Luis Obispo. The call advised them that Jill could be found at a bed and breakfast by the name of Petit Soleil Bed and Breakfast. The San Luis Obispo police searched the small establishment, and found her in her room. She was unconscious, having attempted to end her life with an overdose , just as she had stated that she would in her email.

It was three days after the initial murder when Jill Rockcastle was finally found and apprehended. After the email had gone out, people had begun coming forward with stories of their experiences with Jill Rockcastle and Bill Gustafik. Some people were adamant that Bill didn't deserve what he had got, even if he was a scammer and a cheat. Many people also described Jill has being aggressive herself, with a cocaine habit that matched her husband's. More and more people came forward to tell their stories about how the couple had cheated them out of property and money.

It was Jill's email that had described Bill as aggressive and dangerous, detailing all of the ways in which she was afraid of him. As more people came out of the woodwork as victim's of Jill and Bill, a new light was beginning to be shed on Jill herself. Jim Rivera, one of Bill Gustafik's closest friends from when they were younger, described the Bill in Jill's letter as "inconsistent" with the man that he had known his whole life. Another anonymous friend, this one of Rockcastle, described Jill has being the one to lure Bill into a relationship. Jill was the mastermind, people who knew the couple said. In court, attorneys said that Jill Rockcastle showed no signs of battered woman's syndrome, as both her own public defender and ten page email tried to claim.

Perhaps no one will ever know the truth of what happened between Bill Gustafik and Jill Rockcastle. All that is known is the memories of the couple, the memories of Bill, and the email that had been sent to friends, family and business contacts. Jill had intended to be dead after sending that email, so there is no telling what is truth, exaggeration, or fiction, when Jill did not expect to have to answer for her crime, or the story that she left behind.

BLACK WIDOW KRISTIN ROSSUM

AIMEE BAXTER

Photos of a beautiful, lively little girl, her blonde hair in pigtails as she dances The Nutcracker in her little pink tutu. That same adorable child laughingly enjoying holidays with her family at their home. These are the pictures that Constance Rossum will show you of her daughter Kristin.

Bright, vivacious, and uncommonly beautiful are the words used to describe Kristin Rossum as a child. The child that everyone said was so smart and pretty, the one who modeled for department stores and who excelled in her schoolwork, the one with what seemed to be the perfect suburban childhood.

However, as many already know ... looks can be deceiving.

Idyllic Child becomes a Rebellious Teen

Born to Ralph and Constance Rossum on October 25, 1976, in Claremont, California, Kristin Rossum wanted for nothing. Kristin was the first child of Ralph Rossum – a professor at Claremont McKenna College – and his wife Constance – who worked at Azusa Pacific University. Even when her first and then second little brother was born, Kristin remained her parent's sweet little princess.

When Ralph accepted a position as President of Hampden-Sydney College in southern Virginia, the family moved across the country from California to Virginia. It was 1991 and Kristin was a delicate 15 years old. Her parents enrolled her in an all-girl boarding school in Richmond, Virginia named St. Catherine's School.

That seems to be the beginning of the end of Kristin's innocence. At the private school, Kristin made friends quickly and soon was very popular. She became the party girl smoking, drinking, and using marijuana liberally.

In 1992, at just 16 years old, Kristin is introduced to methamphetamines – a strong Central Nervous System (CNS) stimulant – and is soon hooked. Within a few weeks, she was using Crystal Meth (also known as Crank, Speed, Chalk, etc.) daily. She was a tweaker (slang used to describe a methamphetamine addict).

Kristin the Druggie

When asked about it later, Kristin recalled her first time using meth by saying "I remember it feeling good, a kind of euphoria. You feel very revved up and energetic and happy. I wanted to feel that all the time."

Soon, Kristin's straight As were slipping to become Cs and Ds. She lost weight rapidly and began to withdraw from her family and any friends who were not using meth. According to later court records, Kristin is described as having "an almost insatiable need for crystal meth."

It was not long before Kristin developed all the character traits that addicts hone to conceal and continue their freedom to use. Lying, manipulation, and theft became the new norm for young Kristin Rossum.

Her parents were understandably at a loss for how to deal with this behavior. After all, not that long ago they were tucking her into her pink canopy bed and kissing her goodnight with a song and a prayer. However, the lack of consequences established by her parents could be a contributing factor in her later misdeeds.

At first, they ignored their daughter's erratic and rapidly devolving character, chalking it up to teenage angst. Eventually, they could not turn a blind eye anymore and they soon realized that their daughter was not who they thought she was.

Later, both Ralph and Constance cite an incident in 1993 as the first time they admitted their daughter had a problem. After returning from a cruise in April of that year, the Rossums found that their sweet, perfect daughter had in fact stolen their credit cards, personal checks, and a video camera.

Confronted with the missing items, Kristin pointed to some of her friends (fellow druggies) as the thieves. They say that she admitted to using some of the cash to buy drugs but insisted that the rest was stolen by somebody else. Her parents accepted Kristin's excuse and did not report the theft to police.

According to Constance's testimony later, Kristin's erratic behavior came to a head in December of 1993. Ralph Rossum – convinced Kristin was still using drugs – attempted to search his daughter's backpack. She resisted, they struggled, and he struck her several times in the arm to get the bag away from her.

However, that was not the end of the incident. Sobbing and enraged, Kristin grabbed a knife from the kitchen and slashed at her wrists. When that did not work, she ran upstairs to the bathroom, locked herself inside, and began hacking at her wrists with a razor. Later Kristin told the court, "I felt devastated ... I didn't know how to deal with the situation ... I wanted them to see how sorry I was."

Her wounds, however, were superficial and her parents treated them at home. They later said that they were "afraid of what would happen if they took her to the hospital." They feared that if they told the hospital that she had cut herself, they would have committed her for a psychiatric evaluation and if they tested her blood and found drugs, they would report her to the police.

It is likely that the reason none of the cuts were serious was that Kristin did not intend them to be. Psychologists later speculated that it was merely a way for her to manipulate her parents. If it was, it worked.

Again, Kristin escaped any immediate consequences for her bad behavior. Again, her parents made excuses for her behavior and thus enable her to continue that behavior. Cryptically, one entry in her diary after this incident contained the morbidly, prophetic words, "I could get away with murder."

A few days after this incident, a teacher noticed the marks on Kristin (or she possibly showed them to her intentionally). She called the police to the school to investigate the possibility of child abuse.

Officer Larry Horowitz of the Claremont Police investigated and testified that Kristin told him that her father had hit her and that her mother had "called her a slut and said she was worthless." After interviewing Ralph and Constance Rossum, Officer Horowitz concluded that there had been no abuse and the case was closed.

In January 1994, Constance found a glass pipe hidden in Kristin's underwear drawer. She eventually called Officer Horowitz and Kristin was handcuffed, arrested, and held for several hours at Claremont Municipal Jail.

Kristin finally had her first taste of culpability. She seemed to clean her act up and after graduating, she enrolled part-time at the University of Redlands in California. However, soon she relapsed and dropped out of school without a word to her family and simply disappeared. She moved to Chula Vista – a suburb of San Diego near the Mexican border.

A Chance Encounter

After a month of hard partying, drinking, smoking meth, and hiding from her parents, Kristin was walking the pedestrian bridge that led from Chula Vista to Tijuana, Mexico. Authorities speculate that at the time she was likely on her way to meet her supplier in Mexico on that fateful day.

As she crossed the bridge, Kristin Rossum dropped her jacket. Before she could retrieve it, a handsome young man that she later described as reminding her of John Stamos, had picked it up and was handing it to her. It was Greg de Villers and he later told friends "it was love at first sight." They chatted in French while Greg's younger brother paced nearby.

She returned to the Southern California apartment where de Villers lived with his brothers, Bertrand and Jerome, and a friend, Christopher Wren. She never left.

Within a few weeks, the couple was professing their love and de Villers had sworn to help Kristin kick her meth addiction. Greg's brothers and Wren were not happy and prompted him to end the relationship. They had noticed that things were coming up missing from the apartment since Kristin's arrival and knew of her drug problem.

According to a statement given later by de Villers' friend and roommate Christopher Wren, Kristin had told him that she felt like being with Greg was the wrong choice. For some reason, Wren chose not to tell his buddy.

Even if Wren had told de Villers about Kristin's doubts, it is unlikely that it would have made any difference. Greg de Villers was adamant, he loved Kristin Rossum no matter what her faults and he was going to save her from herself.

By May of 1995, it looked as though he had done just that. By all accounts, it looked like Kristin was clean and free of the hold meth had on her. She reestablished contact with her worried parents and it looked like Kristin was finally moving towards the bright future her parents had envisioned for their little girl.

The Rossums looked at Greg de Villers as if he was an angel for all that he had done for Kristin. Constance Rossum, in an interview with the CBS news magazine "48 Hours," put it like this, "We always called Greg our godsend from heaven. I mean, of all the people she could have met, to have met a nice, decent person who wanted to take care of her, we thanked God."

Soon, Kristin enrolled at San Diego State University. Her professors later said described Rossum as a stellar student with one going so far as to describe her as "among the most promising students" he had "ever taught."

Everyone who knew her believed she was happy. She was earning straight As and in 1998, she graduated cum laude (with honors). She got a job at San Diego Medical Examiner's office as a toxicologist.

Constance would later testify, "Our old Kristin was back," and she thanked God and de Villers – in that order – for the change.

Storybook Love?

Everyone who knew them described Kristin and Greg as the perfect couple. Constance Rossum testified later that when they were together they were "like a couple of lovebirds." When they announced their engagement, nobody was surprised.

However, as is often the case, outward appearances did not accurately represent reality. There was a layer of tension beneath the surface of de Villers and Rossum's storybook love affair. Kristin's closest friends knew that she had a hard time staying faithful and monogamous.

According to prosecutor's later, Kristin actually maintained a "graphically flirtatious" correspondence with a former boyfriend and at least one other man during at least some portion of her relationship with de Villers. Rossum even went to her mother only a month before she was supposed to walk down the aisle and broke down in tears as she told her mother that she wanted to cancel the wedding.

Constance Rossum considered her daughter's outburst to be cold feet, pre-wedding jitters that would pass. After all, Greg de Villers was the man who led her out of the darkness of addiction and Constance could not see how Kristin could possibly want to end the relationship.

She would soon tell the court, "I gave her the wrong counsel, I'm afraid."

The wedding was spectacular. The video shows a smiling and laughing Kristin Rossum, now Kristin de Villers, dancing with her new husband and looking happy. As for de Villers, he is recorded on that video saying, "Kristin is the most wonderful person I've ever met. I just can't wait to spend the rest of my life with her."

Only seven months after the wedding, however, Kristin Rossum told her mother that she felt "trapped like a bird in a cage." It was January 2000 and Kristin's journal shows that she had begun souring on her marriage only a couple of months after the wedding.

Greg de Villers did not show any sign that he felt the same or even knew of his wife's misgivings and doubt. Conversely, his brother Jerome later testified that Greg was ecstatically happy and never spoke of anything even smacking of marital discord. Even his colleagues at a genetics research firm where de Villers worked, described him as happily married and devoted to his wife. Some even went so far as to describe Greg de Villers as "sickeningly in love with his wife."

Friends of Greg de Villers said that he was often talking about his plans for their future together. He bragged about his wife's accomplishments, both big and small, and often spoke of starting a family. One friend remembers him saying that he wanted "all girls who were as beautiful and smart as Kristin."

At the same time, his adored wife was painting a much grimmer portrait of her marriage and her husband. She often complained to colleagues and friends about Greg, saying that he was moody, controlling, and domineering. Later, in an interview with "48 Hours," Kristin said, "Greg became very, very clinging... I tried to pull away and have some sort of independence."

An email sent to her brother Brent only 11 months after the wedding showed how she truly felt. She wrote, "I should have trusted my own instincts and called off the wedding. Now I'm stuck with the heavy realization that I married the wrong person."

A New Love Affair

Not long after Kristin Rossum sent that email to her brother, she met Dr. Michael Robertson. Newly hired as Chief Toxicologist at the San Diego Medical Examiner's office, Robertson was Kristin's immediate supervisor and she began spending large amounts of time with him.

Soon, they were spending time together outside of work. Kristin found danger and excitement in her passionate affair with her handsome, Australian doctor – who was also married. Her husband – and the problems she seemed to have with him – disappeared from Kristin's consideration and soon she was talking with friends outside of her colleagues about the wonderful new man in her life who she described as "a big hunk of an Australian guy."

By early May, Rossum was receiving inappropriate emails and notes from her boss. A search of her desk later turned up love notes and IOUs for things such as "a night of lovemaking" from Robertson. Coworkers later reported that Robertson was often seen sauntering into work with a bouquet of flowers that would soon end up on Rossum's desk.

In June, according to court records, Kristin Rossum had given her lover a gift. A book titled "52 Invitations To Great Sex" she had inscribed on the inside cover, "Well, sweetheart, together we'll enjoy a lifetime of passion."

When asked later, Rossum said, "I felt like I was in love. It was very romantic, very exciting, very passionate."

In August of 2000, Kristin turned to her best friend, Melissa Prager. Prager later told the court that he friend confided in her that she was madly in love with Robertson but was "terrified" by the idea of telling Greg she wanted a divorce.

In October 2000, Greg de Villers was still telling his friends, family, co-workers, and anyone else who would listen about his love for his wife and his plans for their future. His brother Jerome later told the court that around Halloween, Greg was talking about his excitement over taking his future children with Kristin out to trick or treat.

However, Kristin Rossum had reached a conclusion about her marriage. She told her close friends that she was looking for an apartment and planned to leave her husband.

'Til Death Do Us Part

It is unclear how de Villers learned of his wife's infidelity and plan to leave him. Rossum has always claimed that she told Greg de Villers about the affair and that her admission launched a spiraling depression in her husband.

According to Kristin Rossum, she told her husband about Robertson and he demanded the man's phone number. When Kristin supplied the number (although why she would is uncertain), de Villers called her boss and lover and demanded that he break off their relationship.

There is no court record of a response to this demand by Robertson. However, the relationship continued.

Authorities, however, have a very different set of circumstances in mind for how Greg discovered Kristin's infidelity.

They maintain that de Villers found out about the affair on accident in the fall of 2000. This was after Kristin and Robertson were sent to Milwaukee together to attend a toxicology conference. According to court records, despite being booked into separate hotels – likely due to rumors in the office about their relationship – the duo rented their own room together and spent several nights from September 30 to October 7 together in that room.

A coworker saw Kristin at the conference during the week and noted that she was no longer wearing her wedding ring.

One of the conferences that Rossum and Robertson attended in Milwaukee was on the deadly effects of fentanyl. Fentanyl is a clear, odorless narcotic that is 100 times stronger than morphine. It is generally administered to cancer patients whose pain is not eased by other means. It is so potent that it only takes a few drops to kill.

The seminar also discussed the fact that the drug is so rarely prescribed and used that most medical examiner's offices do not test for it. Both Rossum and Robertson were well aware of the fact that their office did not test for fentanyl.

During the three years that Rossum had worked in the San Diego Medical Examiner's office, only seven cases of death by overdose had involved fentanyl. She had seen 15 patches and 1 vial of the drug in a powder form. It was Rossum's job to log and track the drugs in her logbook. It was Robertson's job to hold the key to the cabinet those substances was then stored in.

These were facts that seemed innocuous at the time but would soon hold a more serious meaning.

Returning to Old Ways

Only a day or two after returning from Milwaukee, Rossum sent de Villers an email telling him that she was taking three different prescription drugs "to help with the severe anxiety I've been experiencing as a result of our relationship. You've hurt me beyond repair."

Not only was Kristin taking prescription medications, she had fallen back into her addiction to meth. After some of the drugs went missing from her office, Robertson admitted later that he found traces of the drug in her desk and rather than turning his girlfriend in, he flushed the drugs down the toilet. Then he covered for her with his superiors.

Once again, Kristin Rossum has done something bad. Once again, somebody shields her from the ramifications of her actions. Once again, there are no consequences for Kristin's bad actions.

Severing Ties

By early November 2000, Rossum was ready to end her relationship with de Villers. She insisted she wanted only a "trial separation."

She later told detectives that de Villers literally collapsed when she told him she was leaving him. She claimed that he lay in bed for days afterward and would not communicate with her. She later told the court, "It was painful for me, too, to see someone you love hurt so much." She still never owned up to the fact that it was her own actions that caused her husband that pain.

On November 6, 2000, just after 9:15 pm, Kristin Rossum called 991.

She claimed that her husband was unresponsive and that she was doing CPR to try and revive him. When paramedics arrived, however, they found Rossum on the phone in the living room. Her husband was lying lifeless on their bed.

Gregory de Villers lay dead in his La Jolla bedroom with rose petals covering his chest. Besides his lifeless head lay a copy of his wedding picture ... less than two years old. Nearby on the floor lay a crumpled love letter from the dashing Australian doctor that was his wife's boss and lover. Beside that was his wife's discarded diary, open to an entry that she had left confiding that she felt her marriage was the biggest mistake of her life.

For all intents and purposes, it looked like a suicide. His distraught widow claimed that Greg had learned that her affair with Robertson was still happening.

However, de Villers' brother Jerome adamantly refused to accept that his brother had committed suicide. The entire de Villers family demanded an investigation. Still, the San Diego police were hesitant to open an investigation.

The Truth and Nothing but the Truth

Their opinion quickly changed and authorities soon came to suspect Kristin Rossum, de Villers' 26-year-old blonde beauty of a wife. They believed that she had used her knowledge as a toxicologist and the information that she had gleaned from working in the medical examiner's office to poison her husband.

Due to concerns over a conflict of interest, de Villers' autopsy was outsourced to another lab in Los Angeles. That lab is one of the few in the country that tests for fentanyl. They found 7 times the lethal dose of fentanyl in de Villers' system.

Two weeks after de Villers' death, the San Diego police brought Kristin Rossum in for interrogation. She reiterated to police that her husband had been extremely depressed.

According to Kristin Rossum's story, on the Thursday before de Villers' death, they struggled over a letter that she had sticking out of her back pocket. In her account, de Villers' attempted to grab the letter from her pocket and knocked her to the ground to wrest it from her. She claimed that it was the first time she had been afraid of her husband.

When he had the letter, as Rossum's story goes, he held it out and threatened to take it to his wife's office and expose the affair as well as her reoccurring meth addiction. She took the letter and shredded it but de Villers pieced it back together.

In court, Rossum's parents described the night, two days before de Villers' death, when they went over to visit the couple for dinner. Ralph Rossum testified that de Villers seemed to be deeply depressed, "a man spiraling down."

Kristin Rossum's father continued to describe how de Villers had drunk heavily that night. He drank wine and gin until his father in law had to tell him to lower his voice. Constance Rossum described

Greg de Villers' voice as "fraught with melodrama" as he spoke at length about the dozen red roses that he had given to Kristin for her birthday a few days earlier.

She testified that he seemed depressed, agitated, and particularly obsessed with the fact that all but one had died and shed its petals. In a TV interview, she gave months after the death, Rossum stated, "He was making a big deal of the last rose standing. I think he was just making a statement that he knew our relationship was over."

Things rapidly spiraled from that point on. Police learned that Rossum had relapsed and was using meth again.

On June 25, 2001 – 7 months after Greg de Villers' death – his wife was arrested on charges of First Degree Murder. She spent over six months in jail and then on January 4, 2002, her parents posted $1.25 million for bail.

During the trial, the prosecution contended that she killed her husband to keep him from telling her bosses that she was having an affair with Robertson and that she was stealing meth from the office. They presented evidence that she had the knowledge about fentanyl to use it, access to the drug (remember the missing fentanyl from her office), and the motive to kill her husband.

On November 12, 2002, Kristin Rossum was found guilty of first-degree murder.

Exactly one month later on December 12, she was sentenced to life in prison without the chance of parole. She was transferred from the San Diego jail to the Central California Women's Facility in Chowchilla California – the largest women's correctional facility in the United States.

Distant Repercussions

In 2006, the de Villers family filed a lawsuit against Rossum and San Diego County for wrongful death. They were asking for $50 million but on March 25, 2006, a San Diego jury ordered Rossum to pay more than $100 million in punitive damages to the de Villers family. The same judge ordered San Diego County to pay $1.5 million.

According to the de Villers' lawyer John Gomez, the punitive damages awarded in this case are the most assessed against an individual defendant in California history. The jury apparently awarded double what the de Villers' family was asking for due to the estimation that Rossum could make $60 million from selling the rights to her story.

The judge later lowered the awarded amounts to $10 million in punitive damages and $4.5 million in a compensatory award.

In September of 2010, a 3-judge panel of the 9th US Circuit Court of Appeals ruled that Rossum's lawyers should have challenged the prosecutions assertion that she poisoned her husband with fentanyl by demanding their own tests. Due to this, the panel ordered a San Diego federal court to hold a hearing into whether the defense's error could have affected the trial's outcome.

On September 13, 2011, the US Court of Appeals withdrew its opinion and replaced it with a one-paragraph statement that denied Rossum's petition.

Conclusion

Kristin Rossum will spend the rest of her life behind bars. She has exhausted her state appeals and the federal courts denied her petition to be heard.

Her contention remains that her husband killed himself. She further believes that he did it the way that he did to point the finger of guilt at her. She vehemently insists that she did not kill her husband.

At one point, Kristin Rossum even suggested that her lover the handsome Australian doctor might have killed her husband. He knew about de Villers' threat to expose them before his death and had access to the fentanyl.

For his part, Robertson returned to Brisbane, Australia only one month after de Villers' death under the excuse that he had to care for his ailing mother. In September of 2013, the San Diego Reader reported that prosecutors filed a criminal complaint against Robertson in 2006 charging him with one count of conspiracy to obstruct justice.

If he returned to the US, Robertson could face up to three years in prison. In 2001, Robertson was named as an "unindicted co-conspirator" in Rossum's trial.

As of 2014, Robertson was running a forensic consulting business in Brisbane.

Kristin Rossum, the sweet spoiled only daughter of college professors, who was never held accountable for her actions as she grew up will spend the rest of her days within the walls of the largest women's correctional facility in the US. She is finally going to have to answer for what she has done.

GWEN HENDRICKS

173

Gwen Gillespie Hendricks was born into a Navy family in Memphis, Tennessee in 1955.

Her father was a naval officer while her mother was a housewife. Like most military families, they moved often from station to station, according to her father's assignment. Growing up in a devoutly Catholic home and Gwen would embrace the religion with fervor.

Gwen dressed with modesty, wearing button down shirts and minimal make-up. She fostered a nerd look, with wire-rimmed glasses and short hair.

Carrying on the family's military tradition, she joined the Air Force at the age of twenty-five. It was there she would meet Jim Hendricks, twenty-four, who was her instructor.

Jim Hendricks was a tall, strapping Air Force sergeant with an air of authority. He had an easy smile and Gwen found him easy on the eyes.

"Well, it was kind of instant attraction," Gwen recalled. "There was a bit of lust there as he's a very tall, handsome man. The Air Force can tell you that you can't date but they can't tell you who to marry so I went to the Jag office and asked if I could marry my STA and they said 'yes.'"

The two were married in 1980. Jim had a five year old daughter, Season Hendricks, from a previous relationship. In 1982, they would have a son, Ben.

Because of their career choice, the couple spent a lot of time apart during the early years of their marriage. Jim was stationed at Wake Island while Gwen was assigned to Eglin Air Force Base in Florida.

The couple would be reunited in 1986 as Jim was assigned to the Air Force Academy in Colorado Springs. Gwen would not re-enlist in the Air Force, instead taking a job with the Internal Revenue Service.

The couple spent three years in Colorado before Jim would be transferred to Guam in August of 1989. He took the the entire family with him to the island.

"I figured we had a pretty normal family," Season said. "Until we moved to Guam. Things started to change. She (Gwen) would pick fights. She was jealous of the time my Dad and I would spend together."

"She (Gwen) had a different life in mind for herself," forensic psychologist Joyce Smith said. "She was used to having her own money. So when they moved to Guam there was little to do and less money to do it with."

Gwen and the children moved back to the United States, returning to Colorado and leaving Jim in Guam.

She would buy a home in Littleton and once again start working for the IRS. She then joined the junior Chamber of Commerce where she met Terry Knaack and a woman named Rochelle.

"Rochelle was into tarot cards," Gwen said. "And Terry was into new age occultism. My religion, my faith was still very meaningful to me. I wanted to do Bible study with them to get them out of what I considered witchcraft. Rochelle said she wouldn't go to Bible study with me unless I did the cards with her and the same with Terry. So I think I opened up the door to hell. Right after I started, everything went wrong"

During this time, Gwen began to experience health issues. She suffered from dizzy spells and nausea.

Her personality shifted as well, changing from being even-tempered to easily agitated and manic. With her health and ability to focus effected, Gwen stepped down from her revenue collector position to tax examiner.

"Could the illness have played a part in her deciding to kill her husband?" Smith asked. "Maybe. But Gwen was really steeped into religion and sounded like she embraced some of the more fringe elements of Christianity. She truly believed that occultism was a form of witchcraft and that those things could do her harm. So when she suffered from her illness she erroneously attributed it to her dabbling in the occult. She was a woman who preferred supernatural explanations to rational thought."

Gwen also started to grow deeper into debt, buying expensive gifts for friends.

In the fall of 1990, Gwen hired Terry Knaack to help remodel the Littleton home. A few months later, Knaack moved into the couple's basement with the rationale being he would be able to help with the mortgage. With the husband away and a man in the home, Gwen began to fantasize about Terry and starting over with him.

"Terry would talk a lot about wanting to having a ranch for children with special needs," Gwen recalled. "And I started having delusions that he and I would start this ranch together for the children."

"She entered into a fantasy world," Smith said. "She began imagining a life with this other man, having delusions of grandeur of what they would do together. He became her willing accomplice in her dreams, since her own husband was absent because of military duty. So an alternate universe with Terry Knaack became her obsession. What probably started as harmless day dreams soon grew into something sinister."

"I also believe that Gwen had more than a little bit of a Messiah complex. She had this compulsion to save people and it manifested in doling out gifts and handouts to people who she felt were in need. She had this secret life and kept things from Jim who was away on military assignment. Those secrets involved getting into credit card debt."

By January of 1991, Gwen began telling friends that she was having premonitions of Jim dying in a plane crash.

"I had this really bad dream over and over again," Gwen recalled. "Where Jim had died in a plane crash. I was thinking, well after Jim died that I would marry Terry and we'd start this ranch but of course Terry didn't know anything about because it was all in my head."

Gwen then began hearing voices.

"They (the voices) wanted me to sacrifice what was most dear in my life," Gwen recalled. "I remember thinking that I have to answer these voices because this is coming from God. You know, I've got to sacrifice what I loved the most and that was Jim."

Gwen kept a journal where she logged the "premonitions" of her husband's death. She titled the journal "The Courage to Will and Persevere," She described the voices that she heard and believed that God had told her to kill Jim.

"She experienced what we call 'command hallucinations,'" said Smith. "These are sometimes coupled with someone's value system, in this case, it was Gwen's religion. Gwen believed that she should obey God and believed that the voices that she heard were, in fact, coming from God. So this could go bad real quick if those voices told her to do damage to someone."

"She was past the breaking point, a delusional schizophrenic that was not diagnosed. When she confided with friends it was probably with people who shared her same point of view, people who believed in visions, messages from God and premonitions. Gwen was a soft-spoken woman and even if someone thought she was crazy they would not think she would be capable of taking a gun and blowing someone's brains out. She didn't have that violent vibe."

But behind closed doors, Gwen would deal with problems or difficulties in a haphazard fashion. She would often open up the Bible and believed that whatever random verse she came upon was a direct message from God.

"I reread Psalm 90 quite a few times before a small voice said, 'Keep reading, keep reading.'" Gwen wrote in her journal. "After reading the first page of stanzas, I knew I would be protected from the car bombs, the knifings, the guns, the contracts and all the other evil I had seen connected with busting the pornographers and pimps. Those mafia guys play rough, but somehow they just won't be able to get me. Then I turned the page to continue reading. It felt like a giant fist had slammed into my heart. I literally could not breath [sic]. I burst into sobs and sunk to the floor. I cried for Jim because he really was going to die."

Gwen began to prepare for Jim's death, taking out a $300,000 life insurance policy on her husband payable on his death.

She then visited a local banker, informing him that she would be soon be receiving proceeds from insurance claim. Gwen was told that she would not be able to use the money as long as Jim was alive. She then forged a doctor's note which alleged that she had multiple sclerosis. She submitted this note to the Red Cross along with a letter stating that they should be responsible for being her husband back from Guam.

Gwen did not want the proceeds from the insurance for her own material gain. She believed that she could use the proceeds from his life insurance to establish the "James Hendricks Foundation" to aid victims of mafia produced pornography.

"She became obsessed with pornographers," Smith said. "Like most people with Messiah Complexes, she chose an ill of society and focused on that, believing that she was a chosen vessel to help eradicate the 'sin'. In her deluded mind, she needed this money to accommodate God's will to establish this ranch wherein she would save victims of pornography. The only way she could attain this goal would be to kill Jim and take the life insurance proceeds."

"I was very desperate to have him (Jim) back," Gwen said. "I felt like I was at my limit and not really realizing that I actually was really having a breakdown."

With her husband not even dead yet, Gwen began purchasing clothes for herself and the children to wear for his funeral.

She bought silk flowers and boxes of Kleenex for mourning friends and family.

Gwen also increased the amount of Jim's life insurance from $300,000 to $1,000,000.

True to her premonition, she bought a wedding dress for herself and put a wedding ring on layaway for Knaack.

Gwen would ask God to speak to her directly and "guide her hand" as she thumbed through her Bible. When she got to a passage, she would believe that was what God wanted her to study."

"For the first reading, only the last sentence made sense," Gwen wrote. *"I had asked if what I felt about Jim's death was real. He said yes.*

God can even speak through the dictionary!

After reading the first page of stanzas, I knew I would be protected from car bombs, the knifings, the guns, the contracts and all the other evil I had seen connected with busting pornographers and pimps. Those Mafia guys play rough, but somehow they just won't be able to get me."

"You can see her delusions of grandeur in her journal writings," Smith said. "She had all of the symptoms of a delusional narcissist, truly believing that God made her as the 'Chosen One.'"

Gwen would write that she had a two-way conversation with God about creating the ranch.

"'Oh, so the ranch is in Douglas county near to the Springs so my family will be protected from the mafia guys' Then I knew in Denver, I'm Gwen Hendricks. In the Springs, I'm Gwen Knaack. I had thought the clinic would carry the name of the ranch, but with this new insight, I knew that for safety sake, everything had to be kept separate."

She continued to have health issues as well, as the nausea and attacks of dizziness still had not subsided. Physicians could not determine the cause of her illness. She was eventually diagnosed with Ménière's disease, an ailment that causes vertigo and a fluctuating hearing loss. She had a micro-shunt placed into her ear which only helped relieve the pain she was experiencing.

Her mental health, however, continued to deteriorate.

Jim would return to Colorado for good in May of 1991. It would not be a well-received reunion, however, as the couple fought over everything specifically the living arrangements of Knaack. Jim promptly kicked the boarder out of the home.

He then took control of the finances as he discovered that Gwen had maxed out the credit cards.

"My brother said that she had apparently taken several other credit cards and had maxed them out to the limit," recalled Steve Hendricks, Jim's brother. "And he was furious with her at that point. He did confide in me that he was thinking about leaving Gwen."

Jim would take away all of Gwen's credit cards and this made her extremely angry.

"He took away her power," Smith said. "She got an ego boost by buying expensive gifts for friends and helping out women that she thought were in need. When Jim took that away, she saw him as someone who needed to be eliminated."

Divorce seemed imminent but Gwen seemed immune to it all in her journal writings.

"The funeral, the ranch school, children, the foundation, always being pushed forward," she wrote. "I have to do what I have to do, too. But just for now I'm going to take one day at a time. I'm hoping I don't get too compulsed to do anything more for at least this coming week. I need to rest.

Perhaps I should start by explaining the little voice. It's my voice, but not me. It comes from somewhere inside, and if I don't listen to it, act on it, it becomes a compulsion. If I don't listen and act on the compulsion, it grows stronger and stronger until it dominates all aspects of my life. I learned long ago to listen and do what I'm told. Things work out when I do, and when I don't, things get real miserable...Yes, my little voice is the way God reaches me with the Holy Spirit."

With Jim now home on a permanent basis, The voices in her head grew louder. They began to speak with more urgency in telling her that she had to kill her husband.

"True to her religious background, she did not interpret auditory hallucinations as a sign of mental illness," Smith said. "Gwen was the kind of woman who took the stories in the Bible literally, seeing herself as a modern day Abraham who heard voices from God. You hear it in the way she describes the voices in her head telling her to sacrifice her husband in the same way the Bible speaks of God telling Abraham to sacrifice his son Isaac."

"I said 'Lord I surrender to you,'" Gwen recalled. "I'm hearing voices from God and this is what God wants and I have to get this from God and if this is what God wants then I have to give it to him. So I went out and I bought a gun"

"The voices in her head told her it was time," Smith said. "And true to her value system, she had to obey. For her religion was not a therapeutic aid because of the way she had viewed it. Her God was a vengeful one, a violent one."

On Friday, August 17th, 1991 Gwen drove to Peterson Air Force Base to meet with her husband, a 75 mile drive, to bring him a change of clothes.

"Jim was working late and he asked me to bring him something to eat." Gwen said.

She had informed police that Jim was working all night to prepare for an inspection but changed his mind.

Gwen wrote in her journal about the incident.

When Jim called to say he was on his way home, I went into shock. I knew the time was at hand. I knew I wasn't really ready. I screamed and cried and raged. Then I asked again, if he was meant to die or was I just suckered into some kind of head game. Benjamin's daddy died. I cried myself to sleep that night. I thought what was I supposed to do with two husbands. God has the oddest sense of humor."

"She told me that she was gonna make a nice little picnic for them," Gwen's step-daughter Season recalled. "They were going to make a night of it and that she wanted him to feel good for his inspection."

Gwen left the home and dropped off both Season and son Ben with a friend. When Gwen arrived at the Air Force base, however, she stated that Jim told her that he was heading home. She maintained that the two then went back home in separate cars.

"His truck was in the lead," Gwen said. "I was in the car behind. I remember being so tired, I told him I can't go on anymore. I just want a quick nap and let's get in the back of the truck."

She said that they traveled in separate cars but she became tired and slept through the night at a rest stop along Interstate 25.

Police, however, believed that Gwen lured Jim to an abandoned stretch of highway with the promise of sex.

The two met at the side of the road and Gwen hesitated when thinking of pulling out the gun. She wanted her husband to go peacefully.

"I took the gun out from underneath the seat of the car," Gwen said. "I got into the truck and laid next to him and when I could feel that he was deeply sleeping that's when I shot him."

Gwen would shoot Jim six times.

"It was like I was outside of myself," Gwen said. "Looking and watching what I was doing. I felt very numb, very cold, like I was on auto-pilot. I got back into my car and I took apart the gun and I was just throwing the parts out the window and just driving around, just in a fog, not knowing what I was doing, where I was going. I stopped at a roadside rest stop. Fell asleep. When I woke up and I didn't know everything that happened."

When Gwen arrived back home that Saturday she began making calls to the police, stating that her husband was missing.

On Monday morning, she called Jim's supervisor who sent out two officers to search for him.

One of his co-workers would find his pickup truck on the side of Highway 83 in Douglas County. His body had been placed in the camper shell in back of his truck.

He had been shot six times in the chest and neck with a small caliber handgun.

Gwen would become the primary suspect.

Police noted that she hardly showed any emotion when they informed her of her husband's death.

"Her state of mind was that of a wife with a missing husband," one of the deputies recalled. "When she was telling a story, she couldn't stick with the same story. And that's a clue, obviously, to law enforcement."

Gwen would then break the news to Jim's daughter, Season.

"Gwen said they found him by the side of the road in his car," Season said. "And that he had been murdered. I don't remember her crying. It was the worst moment of my life."

Terry Knaack would be helpful in the case against Gwen. She had been secretly in love with him and given him her diary. He read through her writings and promptly delivered the diary to the Douglas County Sheriff's Department. The sheriffs then instructed him to call Gwen while they would listen in.

Gwen would tell Knaack that she didn't kill Jim but that she wanted to die. Then Douglas County Sheriff's Department Kim Castellano's intuition told her something was wrong. The Hendricks had two pre-teens, a boy and a girl and the boy was never around during questioning.

Castellano believed that Gwen had a problem with males. With one of the male investigators, an Air Force official, by her side, Castellano went back to talk to Gwen.

Once again, the boy was not there. Gwen was overly polite to Castellano, asking her if she wanted anything to eat and jumping up to fix her something before she could answer.

Gwen would totally ignored the male detective.

Castellano used this knowledge to her advantage and befriended Gwen, sensing that the delusional woman would be much more forthcoming with a female officer than a male.

Gwen began trusting her enough that she asked for Castellano's help in balancing her check book. The detective then saw that Hendricks had recently taken out several insurance policies that would be hers when her husband died.

The investigators then used a technique police refer to as the "midnight confession." Castellano and the Air Force official went over to the Hendricks house at eleven at night, waking Gwen up.

Questioning her in the family room, Gwen continued to deny her involvement in her husband's killing. Castellano and her partner then took turns reading from Gwen's journal, tightening the screws on her denial. They also saw Jim's watch on the counter.

Castellano then told her to get dressed and that she was being taken in.

Gwen finally cracked. She curled into a fetal position and confessed.

"Two stories that night—the story of the rest area and the story of Highway 83," she sobbed.

Gwen would go on to describe the highway story.

"There is blood everywhere, I can see it everywhere," she said. "It's terrible. My mind won't let me remember. I don't know if I shot him or not. I don't know what's real anymore."

Gwen was then taken to a local hospital where she stayed for two days for a mental health evaluation. She was arrested upon release and charged with her husband's murder.

After undergoing another mental health examination, Gwen was deemed delusional but understood the charges being levied against her.

Because of this, she was found fit to stand trial.

In court, however, Gwen continued to state that she didn't kill her husband. She said that the body found at the crime scene was not Jim's.

"There was the obvious choice for her attorneys to declare her insane," Smith said. "She had one hell of an imagination and could make things up on the fly. She said during the trial that she became completely convinced that her husband was still alive, going into full blown denial. 'He's still alive, he's out there somewhere and you have to find him', she would say. She was completely delusional."

Her first attorney, Lloyd Boyer, stated that it was physically impossible for Gwen to have murdered Jim Hendricks.

"The lack of gunshot residue inside the Capitol (Jim's car) vehicle," Boyer said. "Indicated that the murder had not occurred in the vehicle. Mr. Hendricks was quite a bit larger than Gwen and she was small, not especially strong and could not have moved the victim into the vehicle."

The investigators failed to produce the gun that Gwen used but the prosecution had another tool at its disposal.

The first link was Jim's watch that they found in Gwen's possession, which showed that she had tampered with the crime scene. The prosecution showed how she was going to use the money from the insurance policies and start a "home for troubled people" that would be near the spot where she killed her husband.

The jury found her guilty of first-degree murder and Hendricks was sentenced to life in prison.

"I just kept my faith that Jim would come rescue me and I would be set free from prison," Gwen said. "Of course, that never happened."

Inside the prison, physicians deemed her to be mentally unfit to be included with the general population and transferred her to the psychiatric unit.

"They got me on anti-psychotics," Gwen said. "And anti-depressants but it wasn't until 1997 that I started having memories of what had happened. At first, it was like just pictures and they hit me like bricks, you know. I killed a great husband and Dad. I robbed Season and Ben of their father. I felt lower than dirt."

She did have help, however, as some legal advocates filed briefs on her behalf, claiming that she had been insane at the time of her trial.

In September of 2000, the Supreme Court of Colorado overturned Gwen's conviction and ordered a new trial.

In April of 2001, a judge ruled that Gwen was not guilty by reason of insanity.

The trial lasted ten minutes.

"She came to terms with what she had done," Smith said. "She had stopped protesting, stop denying and admitted to what she had done."

Gwen was then remanded to a psychiatric care facility in Colorado. She then decided to change her name to "Emi Masai".

"When I lost Jim," Gwen said. "I also lost my children. I longed to be a wife and mother again. I redefined myself as married to Christ and being a mother to all the people I meet."

"By renaming herself she thought that she could obtain a new identity," Smith said. "It was a way of divorcing herself from her past transgressions."

Gwen went through four years of psychiatric treatment where the physicians determined that she was no longer a threat to society. She was released to a residential program where she now helps the needy at Mercy Ministries.

She continues to take her anti-psychotic medication.

"I never want to slip back into mental illness again," Gwen said. "I literally thank God every morning I open my medicine cabinet. I've always said justice wasn't done. Justice in this case would have been my execution. A life for a life. But it's not about fairness. It's about recognizing mental illness and knowing that you're not responsible for what you are doing when you're psychotic."

Gwen has had minimal contact with both her son and step-daughter since she committed the murder of their father.

"I long to see them but they let it be known through family channels that they don't want to see me," Gwen said. "So I respect that."

"I'm really glad that Gwen has helped herself enough to admit what she's done," Season said. "And I hope there never is a time where it gets easy for her to look in the mirror. Because there's never a time where it's easy to be without our Dad."

"I wish I could take it back," Gwen said. "Be a good wife and Mom again. I can't turn the clock back. So all I can do is give them my deepest apology and ask them to forgive me."